ENJOY STRESS

ENJOY STRESS

READY?
GET POWER!
SEARCHING FOR USABLE SIMPLICITY?
DON'T DROWN IN ADVICE AND DETAILS.

STANLEY E. ABBOTT

Rev. date: 02/11/2016

To order additional copies of this book, contact:
Xlibris
1-888-795-4274
www.Xlibris.com
Orders@Xlibris.com
732670

CONTENTS

FOREWORD

I have to be honest with you . . . *I hate acronyms!* It goes back to the early days of my career when I worked for the California Department of Transportation (FWY OPS/Caltrans). That experience was reinforced by a stint with the United States Air Force (19CES/LRAFB/SAC/USAF) and later compounded through a variety of positions, in both public and private organizations, all of which seemed determined to out-acronym the others (including SCAG, OCAPCD, SBCO, EMA, etc.). With every advancing step in my career, I had to learn a new secret language based on different and unique interpretations and applications of a host of acronyms. Now this trend is multiplying exponentially with the advent of digital messaging (Twitter, texting, etc.) that has introduced a whole new language based on acronyms, abbreviations, and intuitive word substitutions (u r L8 FO F2F!).

I really object to the way we are squeezing the life out of our words, settling, instead, for a dry residue of letters, numbers, and symbols that cuts us off from the essence of clear, concise, and comprehensive communication; a trend that separates us from the soul of meaning. We have become lazy with our use of language, substituting the economy of messaging for the nuance and precision of a rich and vibrant vocabulary of communication.

Stan Abbott had asked me to review his work on *stress* and then write a *foreword*. And that's what I agreed to do. So when his manuscript hit my inbox, what was the first thing I saw? That's right . . . *acronyms!* *OMG!*

Well, after the paramedics left and my heartbeat and blood pressure returned to something approaching normal, I was still obliged to look beyond the acronyms to see what Stan has to tell us about managing stress. So bear with me as together we peek behind the curtain of acronyms to see what Stan has to say that can help us better cope in this compounding world of rapid *change* and unsustainable levels of *stress*.

In our consulting practice, we see more and more of our clients who are running on empty. They report feeling exhausted, subject to physical, emotional, and functional collapse. They are on the edge of burnout. But this is not surprising, is it? We all recognize what's going on across our busy society . . . we are trying to do too much with too little time and too few resources. And this is manifest in the build up of day-to-day tensions and irritations (*cumulative stress*) that contributes to the symptoms of burnout we see at work, at home, in our schools, on our highways, and across our communities.

However, that is only one part of the *stress* equation. Cumulative stress forms a background, or base-level, that is added to whenever some significant disruption occurs in our life trajectory (*traumatic stress*). These disruptions, or what we refer to as *turning points*, can create opportunities for proactive change but at a price. And that price is measured in the stress that goes along with working our way through unknown and unanticipated territory. Unfortunately, the addition of traumatic stress to the background-level of cumulative stress can, and often does, result in a reduction in job performance and plays havoc with relationships at work and at home. And it generates impacts that can lead to serious physical and mental health problems. My work with clients who are experiencing some crisis in their professional lives tells me that most understand the source of their stress. But they do not have the tools or the techniques needed to manage the turning points in their careers, nor are they taking the time required on an ongoing basis to relieve the cumulative stress that slowly builds up, relief that would provide some extra capacity to deal with episodes of traumatic stress when they come along. And as a result, it takes a lesser incident for them to trip over the redline of traumatic stress, thereby raising the level of additive stress to unmanageable proportions. In a nutshell, we all are faced with too much stress and have too few relief mechanisms at hand with which to cope.

Stress, of course, is not a new phenomenon. It is a natural and pervasive part of the human experience, and has been from the beginning. (Want to know about stress? Try having God throw you out of the Garden of Eden into an inhospitable world populated by lions and tigers and bears, oh my!) And let's not forget that stress plays a positive role in our lives, providing internal signals of danger and motivating us to higher and higher levels of performance. What is different today, however, is the high-level of cumulative stress that we are experiencing plus the repetitious frequency with which traumatic episodes of stress seem to be occurring.

We don't need to dwell on the stress factors we are facing in the modern world. I'm sure you are well aware of the tension and strain that permeate most every aspect of life today. By any measure we might use, the world is changing. Not only are we faced with a world of continuous change, but the pace of that change *is accelerating*. And with change comes stress, lots of stress. (You actually can quantify the magnitude of stress in contemporary society by measuring the shelf space at your local bookstore that is given over to the subject. Try it!)

In our career coaching, we deal with busy people in a busy world. We often see managers who think they just need a bit of help to *reduce* their stress levels. Many think they just need to have a few tools in their kit that will make the stress go away. But if we recognize stress as an important and pervasive part of the human experience, then what we really need are *practical* tools and techniques that can help us *manage* stress so as to get the most from the pressures of contemporary life. Just as we need good coaching to get the best from our physical exercise if we are to maintain good physical health, so also do we need good coaching in the techniques of dealing with stress if we are to maintain a healthy life balance that includes normal and proactive levels of stress. And that's where Stan Abbott's work comes into play.

So what's different about Stan's work on stress? What does he offer that is compelling enough to get me to push aside the curtain of acronyms and try his tools and techniques in my own life and in our management consulting practice? And where should I look to find Stan's work among the myriad of other books that purport to have something significant to offer on the subject of stress and stress relief? Very simply put, we find Stan's work filed under "P" for practical.

That's right, practical. What Stan Abbott gives us is *not* an empirically based study of trends in the occurrence of stress in contemporary society. It is *not* a theoretical treatise that arises from the growing field of cognitive science. It is *not* an economic analysis of the impacts of stress of productivity rates in the workplace. It *is* drawn from his personal experience and lessons learned. It comes from Stan's involvement in managing the stress of a traumatic medical occurrence in his family. It is the tool kit Stan has designed coming out of that experience, and from which we all can draw in identifying and treating the symptoms of cumulative stress, as well as the additive pressures of traumatic stress. What Stan gives us is a practical guide for dealing with the stress factors that plague our contemporary society. It speaks directly to the needs we all have for finding the right set of tools and techniques that will provide us with the stress related balance necessary for attaining a healthy and productive lifestyle.

I found that the value in what Stan gives us comes from the connection his narrative made with my own personal experiences with, and ideas about, stress. For me, the tools in his kit triggered and amplified my own concepts and ideas about stress and stress management. This is the kind of narrative that speaks to each of us individually. This means what I take from the work may be quite different from what you will find. And that is perhaps its greatest contribution. In speaking differently to each of us, Stan reaches out with an individualized message that can be applied for maximum affect across the widest possible audience. Some of the key takeaways that resonate with *me* as being practical, and which I am employing in one form or another in my own life and consulting practice, include:

- *Stress management is intensely personal.* There is no one-size fits all solution to effectively managing stress. We are all individuals with different circumstances, personalities, and resources when it comes to dealing with stress, and each of us must find the right combination of tools and techniques to employ in any given situation. What works for me very likely will not work for you. And what works for me today probably will not work again tomorrow. We need a comprehensive set of tools and techniques that we can draw from in managing our stress levels day by day.

- *Stress management is not the same as stress reduction.* A certain degree of stress is part of a healthy life balance, functioning as a natural alarm for when danger arises and as a mechanism for self-motivation that can help us attain our goals and objectives. Stress management is concerned with finding the right balance for each of us. And that includes a healthy level of stress for personal protection and self-motivation.

- *Managing stress is a future-directed activity.* To be effective in managing the stress in your life, you must have some picture or sense of where you want your life to go as you look to the future. Only by looking ahead can you assemble the right set of tools and techniques for managing stress and producing a life balance that includes the right element of stress that fuels the drive to attain your goals.

- *Long-term success in managing stress requires some means of mutual support and accountability.* Stress management is an exercise in continuous behavioural modification. And this happens best when done with the ongoing support and encouragement of an *accountability partner.* From the outset, you need to share your experience with someone you trust, someone who will hold you accountable for selecting and employing the right tools and techniques for achieving your desired life balance, including a positive and proactive level of stress.

- *Acronyms can be your friends.* I have come to appreciate Stan's particular use of acronyms as a *mnemonic device* for explaining and embedding his central thesis regarding stress management. (Surprise! Surprise!) I found that his use of acronyms is quite effective in giving us the set of tools we need if we are to be proactive in managing stress in our complex and ever-changing world.

- *Enjoy your stress.* Focus on enjoying your stress, not eliminating it. Approach the task of stress management with humor! The more you can smile in the midst of what may seem to be insurmountable pressure, the more the negative energy that goes with uncontrolled stress will turn to positive energy, allowing you to take charge and move proactively toward achieving your life goals and objectives.

- *Stress opens the door for change.* When I am experiencing a period of unusual stress, it invariably means that something is going on in my life that needs to be changed. And if I can locate the source of that stress, I can identify what I need to change. And an analysis of that stress usually gives me the clues required to set some positive and proactive change in motion.

- *Simplify your life—it's just STUFF!* The more you can simplify your life, the more control you will have in managing your stress. Negative, unproductive stress generally is related to an accumulation of acquisitive desires, our natural human response to our need to fulfill basic needs *plus* our heightened desires for comfort, convenience, and luxury that are very much an inbred part of our contemporary society. (Just look at the level of personal debt we carry, especially the burden of credit card debt, and you will understand what I'm talking about!)

Stress is a natural part of the human condition. We are designed with built-in mechanisms that keep us alert to danger and motivate us to protect and provide for ourselves, our families, and our communities. And stress has played a very effective role in our ability as a human species to emerge from the African savannas and populate the four corners of the earth.

However, these mechanisms are more finely tuned to respond to the dangers of the wild than to the dangers of Wall Street. Since the advent of the industrial revolution, the role of stress in our lives seems to have crossed over from positive and proactive to negative and defensive. We need to take a new look at stress, what it means in a highly developed and hyper productive socioeconomic setting. We need to find ways to balance our lives such that stress serves as the alert mechanism for a whole new set of dangers that arise from a highly integrated society that keeps us competing for power and position in a world of increasingly scarce resources.

And this is where the work of Stan Abbott really comes into the picture. He introduces us to a framework that will prepare us to be R.E.A.D.Y. to exercise P.O.W.E.R over the stress in our lives. He takes his own experience and applies it in a way that will trigger additional thoughts about the stress in our own lives. And it points us toward the tools and techniques we need in order to incorporate stress (both cumulative and traumatic) as a positive and proactive part of a balanced lifestyle.

This is not a one-size-fits-all solution. But there is something here for everyone, something to take away and make stress management more effective for you in meeting your particular needs. Stan has shared his learning with us. Now it's up to us to take those learnings and make them our own. Then it is our ongoing responsibility to pass along what we have learned. Stress management is not an individual exercise. It takes a village to support one another in finding the right balance of stress in our lives, a balance that is appropriate to the needs of a twenty-first-century world. I hope you will practice what Stan has given us and then pass it on.

And keep smiling! Humor is a powerful ingredient in stress management, so make use of it whenever it is appropriate. Remember, none of us is going to get out of this alive, so keep things in perspective.

Waylon Jennings, the late Country and Western artist, had a song that I've always liked, especially the line that says, "I've always been crazy, but it's kept me from going insane." Think about it next time you feel overburdened by stress. Laugh a little and then look at what your stress is telling you about your need to change. Then open up this book, get together with someone you trust, and go to work.

I wish you a good journey into the future, one in which your stress plays a positive and proactive role.

Cheers,

F. G. (Sandy) Scott
True North Consultants, Inc.
Stratford, Ontario, Canada
http://newdirectionsinmanagement.com

INTRODUCTION

> *"Opportunities to find deeper powers within ourselves come when life seems most challenging." - Joseph Campbell*

A major facet of my thinking is: how can we simplify the methods so we can deal with natural stress in our lives? I felt personally that coping with stress just had to be simplified. Bookshelves abound with volumes looking at, and giving advice on, coping with stress. This guidebook is the result of my endeavor to answer the call to simplify this mess of data and approach. This simplification could lead to a better understanding of stress itself. More importantly, it gives you great potential to cope with stress.

I also felt that, in addition to being simplified, coping with stress should be *fun*. Why not *enjoy* the adventure! Well coped with stress can lead you to an inventive and vibrant conclusion. You'll be imaginative and productive! I said to myself, "Why not enjoy this success!"

But sorrowfully, many people lose their ability to cope with daily stresses. They may have been successfully lucky up to the very point of losing it. People can also fail to recognize their success in coping. They just do it and do not recognize there is also *joy* in successful coping!

THE ANATOMY OF STRESS

Is stress permeating your life? Why not enjoy your stress? We can thrive and be creative in this enjoyment. Yes, the wallop of uncoped stress can have extremely surprising, overwhelming, and negative involvement upon your mind and body. But getting ready for stress can be your aim!

A major stress situation can also easily allow what is known as cumulative stress. Cumulative stress is caused by the little things (you know—like bad drivers, long checkout lanes, etc.) which build up and lead to a stinking, dreadful, or distressing summary feeling by the end of the day: an overall feeling only you could describe.

Stress is intensely personal. It is yours alone! In order to begin understanding what is going on with stress in your life you need to grasp and accept certain signals which pertain to you, and you alone. The following signals are set as examples to indicate your need for the processes in this guidebook.

PHYSICAL SIGNALS: (There are many more—discover yours!)

- High blood pressure (If you don't know, find out!)
- Muscle spasms or tics
- Frequent headaches
- Alcohol, caffeine, or drug abuse
- Feeling constantly fatigued or burned out
- Running a tune over and over in your head
- Chronic diarrhea or constipation
- Suppressed or persistent sexual frigidity or impotence
- I'm sure you can personalize your particular list

MENTAL SIGNALS: (Only you can discover these—you'll know)

- Not able to have a good laugh and nothing seems funny
- Fear of failure or fear of success
- Cannot effectively concentrate for any length of time
- Suppressed anger (grinding teeth)
- Constant feeling of unease
- Paranoid (that s.o.b. is out to get me)
- I'm sure you can personalize your particular list

How well is your mind and body communicating to you? Our entire mental and physical systems are beautifully designed to adjust and adapt to stress. We need stress to stay vibrant and operate at peak efficiency.

However, we can unfortunately cross over a critical point and have too much stress with which to cope. We are just not prepared! Suddenly, your coping skills seem to have weakened or failed, and you might say, "I am having trouble overcoming things I thought I liked." This is called distress. The uncorrected severe distress can lead to poor job performance, job burnout, early aging, relationship breakdown, or even more destructively, organ damage, and death may result. The medical definition of no stress is death!

This is a major problem for someone who has chosen a high stress profession. This would be especially true if you choose a profession in which stressful situations come in waves and are not metered out equally every day.

Without a well-practiced plan of escape valves and techniques, your reaction to high stress may be to turn into someone you might not recognize. A change in your behavior could result in reactions quite unwanted and unbecoming to you.

REACTION SIGNALS: (Again, these are samples—can you define yours?

- You put people down. This may be momentarily enjoyable, but new problems are generally created: you may feel guilty; you may create unwanted new problems; you may face unexpected consequences from the person you just put down; plus, you don't solve the situation that upsets you.
- You transfer the anger to your roommate, spouse, children, pet, or friends. Why would you do that? Maybe it is because they are available and will still love you anyway. However, the effects of transferring your stress to them may increase your distress as you only escalate the situation to your personal life. You also do not solve the problem. This group can comfort you—but can't solve the problem.

- You accumulate distress in your body and/or attack the body through the abuse of drugs, alcohol, or diet/hygiene. The list of targets is very familiar: Digestive tract disorders; reproductive organ disorders (changed menstrual period and impotence); kidney and bladder problems; skin outbreaks; brain problems (emotional changes, anxiety, depression, etc.); mouth problems (teeth, due to poor hygiene); lung problems (asthma worsens); muscular disorders (normal coordination lessens); and heart problems (attacks of angina and change in rate/rhythm). Plus, an already weakened heart can suffer permanent damage or failure.

This guidebook is designed to simplify and calm down your thinking and approach your stresses through the use of acronyms.

Do you currently feel you are coping well in your life? If you do not feel you are coping well, I would encourage you to read on and enjoy the calm organized processes of thinking and functioning found in this guidebook. If you feel in control of your stresses, potentially your desire is to prepare for your future. Maybe you sincerely wish to educate yourself. Read on.

> *"Foresight turns out to be a critical strategy in times of great stress."*
> *- Jamais Cascio*

THE ENJOYMENT OF STRESS

I am convinced that using this Enjoy Stress guide will not only simplify your thinking, organization, and result. It can be fun as well. We know life can be cluttered, unmapped, and stressful. The Joseph Campbell quote is right. Finding deeper powers is challenging. Jamais Cascio also says it correctly. Wouldn't it be wonderful to simplify the challenge through your foresight to apply the R.E.A.D.Y. for P.O.W.E.R. acronyms in this guide?

Stress management Web sites, books, and friendly advice frustrate me and a whole lot of people. Why? When people are faced with a life or job partnership which has challenging stress circumstances, they really do not know how to use what they know or even how to accumulate and use effective strategies.

Since 1985, I have been educating, conducting workshops, holding seminars, and researching how to simplify the manner in which a person can proceed. The following guide is the result. Sticking to the simple acronyms and all their influence will train you for both chronic and occasionally acute challenging stress circumstances. I have had fun, growth, and success using the acronyms in this guidebook; I'm positive you will too.

What is an acronym? The world is just full of them. Examples would be comparable to WAC from Women's Army Corps, IRS from Internal Revenue Service, or FBI from Federal Bureau of Investigation. The acronym is defined as a word formed from the initial letters or syllables taken from a group of words that form the name of a company, product, or process.

Having zero stress is not good. Why? I have discovered that the medical profession defines zero stress simply in one word: death. So you actually want stress! Isn't that just a bit strange? How can this be right? Because stress is always there: you are, after all, still alive! If you are stressed, be thankful. Oops—you might wonder—why? Stress, properly coped with, can produce a very creative, rich, and likable you! So why not gather a few healthy coping skills to counterbalance your stresses?

Stress has two basic definitions. Bad stress is called distress (unhealthy coping with *bad* events—death in the family, bad boss, etc.). Good stress is called eustress (unhealthy coping with *good* events—marriage, falling in love, etc.). Both can be enjoyed with healthy coping strategies which keep you and your life in equilibrium.

This symmetry is raised by using R.E.A.D.Y. for P.O.W.E.R. strategy. Regardless of your personality type, you are going to love this plan.

The whole world, everyone, is subject to life's stressful events. Still, it's a strange irony people react differently to individual cases. In the same situation or set of circumstances, one person can react positively, while another person can react negatively. These two people at that time have two vastly different levels of coping. One can cope. The other can't. Your coping strategies, suddenly reduced, can create distress.

I believe working the R.E.A.D.Y. for P.O.W.E.R. program conscientiously and steadily will allow a set of strong coping strategies to become habitual. Please don't squander time on fruitless self-accusations or dissatisfied feelings. This will lead to emotions of annoyance, anger, resentfulness, and defeat. These feelings, if left to fester, can even accumulate and make matters worse. You will not be well. Stress can cause sickness. There are many studies that show you may even have the possibility of losing proper function of an organ.

I certainly hope you are motivated to use the strategies in this guide. Simply using the conscious discipline of the acronyms shown in this guide will change your life!

---

*"The perfect **no-stress** environment is the grave. When we change our perception we gain control. The **stress** becomes a challenge, not a threat. When we commit to action, to actually do something rather than feeling trapped by events, the **stress** in our life becomes manageable." – Greg Anderson*

COMMIT TO ACTION

A vast amount of available detailed analysis concerning stress exists in book and Internet form. All of this is available to you with just a small effort. *The purpose of this guidebook is quite different.* It is designed to coordinate and simplify your thoughts, approach, and strategies. Books, essays and Web sites are out there for your research.

This guide is designed for those seeking relief from distress: a possible result of unhealthy coping with stress in your life. You actually need stress to be vibrant and move ahead with trust. It is distress you clearly do not want. Distress is caused by sudden weakness in your otherwise normal coping. This is due to what is often called poor coping skills. This guide will discuss them as healthy coping strategies. This means you must have a work plan to strengthen your coping skills. R.E.A.D.Y. for P.O.W.E.R. is a *simple* plan. A listing of recommended resources is at the end of the guide.

Your responsibility is also rather simple. Make the plan part of your thinking every day. Therefore, you will eventually form habit patterns which mature and become normal activity. In this guide there are ten short chapters in which you will experience definitions and strategies relating to each of the acronyms used.

Developing short- and long-term goals is a real important measure to build your entire procedure simple and direct.

Before you begin, think about and consider the framework of your goals. This is soon to become your journey. You must entrust to this broad design, driven by motivation and focus. You'll need a mission to drive your ambition. You will need targets by which you can systematically analyze progress. You will need to set your journey.

This alone can seem fairly rigorous on the surface. But interestingly, that job is simple as well. Arriving at a path you wish to pursue motivates everything else.

You may have already delved into books, sites, or advice concerning stress in your life. This Enjoy Stress guide will show you how to proceed simply. It is dedicated entirely to organizing and planning your thinking.

What follows is a simple, workable, and easy to think of strategy which trains you in the use of easy to remember acronyms. The acronyms are R.E.A.D.Y. for P.O.W.E.R. The results and the progress using these acronyms will be up to you. Use them regularly over a point of time and you will notice fantastic and measurable progress.

THE ACRONYMS

R.E.A.D.Y.

Relaxation: You learn professional relaxation systems that work.

Exercise: You cross-train thirty minutes three times a week.

Attitude: You are what you think just as 'You are what you eat.'

Diet: You can eat in unhealthy ways or you can eat in healthy ways.

Yield: The first four involve only you. Now we deal with others. That can often be very difficult. There are inventive strategies you can employ to make it fun communicating with them.

P.O.W.E.R.

Persistence: You learn that perseverance can be to your advantage.

Opportunity: You learn to focus upon and recognize/create opportunities.

Wellness: You can be R.E.A.D.Y. because you are well. The strength of your wellness should stay as high as possible for you and your career to survive and thrive with the use of the P.O.W.E.R. acronym.

Energy: You learn to sell yourself as an energetic, vibrant person.

Role: You learn to gain mastery of your role at work and at home.

I certainly hope you are motivated to use the strategies in this guide. The enjoyment of your stresses is the goal. Simply using a plan, a discipline, of acronyms shown in this guide will change your life! After making your plan, you can easily carry them in your head effectively and automatically using them.

Are you R.E.A.D.Y. for P.O.W.E.R.? Will you Enjoy Stress? Yes! It's simple and fun! Stanley E. Abbott

ONE: FRAME YOUR JOURNEY

> *"Life's challenges are not supposed to paralyze you, they're supposed to help you discover who you are." - Bernice Johnson Reagon*

This may be the most fun, and at the same time, the most challenging but important aspect of the whole system of acronyms. But this aspect is a duty which will successfully lead you to the enjoyment of the natural and *wanted* stress you will automatically encounter.

Why is this true? What you achieve in life depends to a very large extent on the objectives you pursue. If you are without a written map of your life's objectives and goals, any storm will whip around your rudderless ship. It is therefore worthwhile to take time to consider if you have worked out and written down solid objectives for yourself. The very act of putting it down forces you to focus on what's important. Your thinking will be more improved, fascinating, and desirable! But please don't confuse wishful thinking with goal setting.

Others can easily manipulate those who don't set their own goals. If we allow ourselves to be bothered and controlled by others, we shouldn't totally blame them, but rather see this as a problem of our own! Decide now to favor yourself. Decide now *not* to be undirected, pointless, or casual.

Your journey begins by framing your goals, aims, objectives, intent, and targets. An obvious way to start is to envision what you want your life to be like. Your life will have control and personal supervision if your journey's mission can energetically motivate the R.E.A.D.Y. for P.O.W.E.R.

strategies in this guidebook. It is time to fill your "tool kit" with your very own set of tools. In doing so, you might find an insight into yourself which is unknown to you at the present.

> *"Many of us feel stress and get overwhelmed not because we're taking on too much, but because we're taking on too little of what really strengthens us." - Marcus Buckingham*

It is a fun task to choose your life goals. Consider what you really want to spend time doing and what really strengthens you. What brings you joy?

Importantly, your ideas cannot exist only in your head; you will have to write down your thoughts on paper. This can be done any way you want. This way there can be ongoing development worked upon, so your mission can be improved on a continuing basis.

Once you are satisfied with your choices and written plan, it would be wise to regularly revisit them so that you can check your progress or adjust and update as necessary. Important and seemingly difficult as this exercise is, you should have fun with your life as well. Plan for fun!

You should expect to succeed. Work and patience will do it!

Expect measurable and immediate success developing this framework if:

- You can work out on paper your life's goals and objectives to pursue! Maybe you'll include others in this process. Anyway, have fun.
- You are willing and able to schedule and use good time management to follow your plan and work the R.E.A.D.Y. for P.O.W.E.R. program.
- You make and take the time to have the resources (include other people) and are able to grow in these coping skills.
- You never forget your motivation!

The past is over and cannot be changed. However, our present and future *can* be managed. This application helps you think about where you are, where you want to be, and what resources you have to get there.

Framing yourself can be expressed and drawn to look any way you want. Formulate a doodle. Doodle in any way that makes sense to you. It is of vital importance you write you down! In this way you are able to consult and modify your framing.

There are several Web sites that can guide you. All you need to do is consult the sites, get an idea of the process, and do it! For illustration purposes you can Google "life map examples". You can then discover, brainstorm, and play around with your doodle. No doubt you will find this exercise fun and fulfilling.

Be positive when you express your goals. For example, instead of saying, "I am *not* going to miss my exercise routine today," write down, "I'll *make time* for a daily 20 minutes on the treadmill."

You can also set goals too low or include other people. This is all about you! Maybe you have said silently to yourself, "I don't really want to volunteer for that project because I might mess it up. And then my colleagues will make fun of me." Allow yourself to think big thoughts. Set your goals in a positive fashion and start working on them! They're also always fluid and adjustable!

Pay attention to everything. Have fun. You can get R.E.A.D.Y. for the P.O.W.E.R. to enjoy stress.

> *"In absence of clearly defined goals, we become strangely loyal to performing daily acts of trivia." - author unknown*

FRAMING TIPS

- Get started and it will be easier to keep going. Believe that you can do it, because you can. Be confident!

- Listen to people whose achievements you respect, and ask for their advice. Remember, you don't have to like the person to respect them.
- Small decisions can have a great impact on working towards your goal. Remember, your newly stated goals keep you from losing your way.
- Good proverbs or sayings can help motivate you. Don't be afraid of using stress-reducing humor. John D. Rockefeller once said, "The secret of success is to get up early, work hard, and strike oil." You must have struck oil! It's called motivation!
- Enjoy pursuing your goals and if they become boring and/or increase your stress levels, then go back and tweak them to allow passion and determination.
- Keep your focus on your issues. Upon starting the journey, you will encounter objections and self-doubt. Be convinced you are on the right path.
- Others can become successful, but you can't? Are they more powerful or deserving than you? No! Never give yourself any excuses, not even one! Otherwise, you will get accustomed to it! You can be successful!
- Working alone makes it harder to receive early and continual feedback, thereby decreasing output quality. A tight feedback cycle is vital to achieving productivity, and the sooner that you can get feedback, the less probable that you'll waste time moving down the wrong way and earlier you'll know to adjust your course. You might find one or more people you trust to work with you not only on framing, but also on your use of the R.E.A.D.Y. for P.O.W.E.R. acronyms.

One of the most difficult behavior modifications humans face is change. For many of us, after we have set a life of action pattern, we do not choose to change. We avoid change. "Why change?" we say. Maybe it looks like too much work. You are apt to say you are under too much stress to change. Maybe just the word "change" evokes too many bad connotations.

Let us look at positive synonyms for the word "change" which may show you how valuable the general concept can be as you develop your journey.

Perhaps you can even adopt the use of one of these words in exchange for the use of the word change: Adjustment. Advance. Development. Diversity. Innovation. Revision. Transformation. Transition. Correction. Refinement. Words have meaning. How you think and use them makes a real difference.

MEMORY

There's a problem with our memories. It doesn't allow us to forget. And that means we actually may lose something of ourselves. Memory can create individual paralysis—because any memory of personal failure is not allowed to fade away. So we aren't encouraged to change and move along.

Recall can freeze us. Memory can easily encourage conformity and a lack of risk taking. When you perform something which results in a failure, memory of that can follow you around forever. So for you, the risk of trying is magnified—so maybe you don't bother trying in the first place. It is anti-creative, anti-experimental, even anti-entrepreneur.

Do what is human nature within you—forget the failures—they were opportunities anyway. Forgetting allows for new beginnings. Every bit a creative medium, a little forgetting goes a long way. Brush it off. Put it in the trash bin. Just do it!

A great quote gets to the point here. "Treat stress like a dog. If you can't eat it or play with it, pee on it and walk away."

TWO: R.E.A.D.Y. OVERVIEW

> *"As a rule, we find what we look for; we achieve what we get ready for."*
> *- James Cash Penney*

Life is a balancing act. Getting ready for the onslaught of various and constantly changing types of stress you will most certainly face is not only a good idea—you will love and enjoy the results.

The R.E.A.D.Y. acronym plan of strategies is designed to help you flourish, avoid sickness, and stay in *balance* on the seesaw and waltz of life. Wellness is certainly your most desired goal. Enjoying your stress will be a byproduct.

Regular use of techniques meaningful to you will most certainly be pleasurable and result in enjoying healthy coping. Each letter in the acronym stands for a *significant* and necessary segment of the total approach.

- **R** stands for **relaxation**

    You'll find that watching television is *not* generally considered relaxation. There are professional programs designed around relaxation as the goal. Practiced regularly three times a week for about a half-hour, these programs are extremely beneficial. Yoga and meditation would be two brief examples among many useful strategies. There are many strategies in this guidebook from which you may select.

- **E** stands for **exercise**

    Exercise leads to better physical fitness, but also develops mental vitality as well. You can learn to avoid the boredom of just one type of exercise. You'll have much more fun with and benefit from cross-training. Regular exercise also provides great mental benefits.

- **A** stands for **attitude**

    Attitude involves only you and your reactions to the external world. No one else is involved in your reactions. Mayo Clinic has identified a few of the many types of negative thinking patterns that could be common to your attitudes:

    1. Catastrophizing is assuming the worst possible result of any eventuality, which is something different from preparing for it.
    2. Filtering is screening out positive aspects of situations, most of which contain *both* positive and negative aspects.
    3. Polarizing is the tendency to classify any outcome as either wholly good or wholly bad (with no middle ground) and setting the standards for a good outcome unrealistically high.
    4. Personalizing is automatically blaming yourself for consequences that aren't necessarily anyone's fault.

- **D** stands for **diet**. You'll find what and when you eat can contribute either to your benefit or to your harm. Healthy food contains natural nutrition, dietary fiber, heart-healthy oils and muscle-building protein not found in processed food loaded with sodium, preservatives, and sugar.

- **Y** stands for **yield**. While yield is often used as a seemingly negative word; you'll find that not true. There are tremendous benefits of using yield strategies that are very positive. To name just a few:

1. Accommodation
2. Cooperation
3. Endorsement

Importantly, yield is the only wellness acronym which specifically deals with how other people react to you, communicate with you, and possibly affect your life negatively. All the other acronyms <u>primarily</u> concern only you. In fact, they spell D.E.A.R.—as in, you can be dear to yourself. This guide adds the **Y**, the yield acronym—now you are R.E.A.D.Y. for all the stresses confronted in life!

> *"If you ask me what the single most important key to longevity is, I would have to say it is avoiding worry, stress and tension. And if you didn't ask me, I'd still have to say it." - George Burns*

THREE: RELAXATION

Relaxation is the first strategy of the **R**.E.A.D.Y. acronym

"Every now and then go away, have a little relaxation, for when you come back to your work, your judgment will be surer." - Leonardo Da Vinci

There are many professional relaxation techniques and strategies found in books and on the Web. Most are very good—some are not. You should pick only the ones that fit you and your enjoyment.

Relaxation is a purposeful technique you have created in order to create decreased anxiety and stress and increased creativity. Meditation, self-hypnosis, prayer, tai chi, and yoga are just a few ideas to pursue. Keep in mind that relaxation also means you could be quite active as well as quiet. There is evidence that vibrant Type A personalities find that skydiving is relaxing. That's odd, but true.

We do know that watching television is generally *not* considered relaxation. The number of times and amount of time spent doing relaxation techniques each week will vary with the strategy selected. Many have chosen several plans for relieving boredom. What technique you choose must work for you!

A few suggestions on professional relaxation techniques are discussed below that can be used to your benefit. They are examples to use as you select your personalized approach.

PROGRESSIVE MUSCLE RELAXATION

There are so many types of these programs. All would be excellent for you. However, you can just pick one. This guide does not delve into specific techniques of progressive muscle relaxation in depth. However, progressive muscle relaxation is an excellent example because of its many benefits. As such, the general nature of this regimen will be discussed below. Check resources at the end of the guide in the appendix for further discoveries you may adopt.

Progressive muscle relaxation is a technique that involves tensing specific muscle groups and then relaxing them to create awareness of tension and relaxation. It is termed progressive because it moves through all major muscle groups, relaxing them one at a time, and eventually leads to total muscle relaxation.

- Assume a passive and comfortable position. You may lie down. Loosen any tight clothing, close your eyes and be quiet.
- Assume a passive, detached attitude. Focus on yourself and on achieving relaxation in specific body muscles. Tune out all other thoughts.
- Tense and relax each muscle group as follows:

  Forehead - Wrinkle your forehead. Relax and repeat. (R&R)
  Eyes/nose - Close eyes tightly for five seconds. R&R.
  Lips, cheeks/jaw - Grimace for five seconds. R&R.
  Hands - Extend arms in front of you, fists clenched. R&R.
  Forearms - Extend arms out in a pushing motion. R&R.
  Upper arms - Bend elbows, biceps tensed. R&R.
  Shoulders - Shrug your shoulders up to your ears. R&R.
  Back - Arch back off floor for five seconds. R&R.
  Stomach - Tighten stomach muscles for five seconds. R&R.
  Hips and buttocks - Tighten hip and buttock muscles. R&R.
  Thighs - Tighten thigh muscles pressing legs together. R&R.
  Feet - Bend ankles toward your body. R&R.
  Toes - Curl your toes as tightly as you can. R&R.

- Focus on muscles which may still be tense. If any muscle remains tense, tighten and relax that specific muscle three or four times.
- Fix the feeling of relaxation in your mind. Resolve to repeat the process again.

Remember, people react differently to various activities. Some feel pleasant or refreshed, and others feel calm and relaxed after an activity like this one. Some people notice little change the first time, but with practice, their control increases—as well as the <u>benefits</u>. Your relaxation should increase when you practice this activity.

CREATIVE VISUALIZATION

Creative visualization refers to the practice of seeking to affect the outer world by changing one's thoughts and expectations. Creative visualization is the basic technique underlying positive thinking and is frequently employed by athletes to enhance their performance. Creative visualization is the technique of using one's <u>imagination</u> to visualize specific behaviors or events occurring in one's life.

You might have seen sports athletes using creative imagination to visualize in advance, with eyes closed, their desired accomplishment of an upcoming athletic event.

Shakti Gawain has said, "Creative visualization can be an effective tool for healing because it goes straight to one source of the problem—your own mental concepts and images." Gawain is a bestselling author and a pioneer in the field of personal growth and consciousness. Her many books, which include *Creative Visualization*, *The Creative Visualization Workbook*, *Creating True Prosperity*, *Developing Intuition*, and *Living in the Light*, have sold more than six million copies in thirty languages worldwide. For over twenty years, she has lead workshops internationally, and has facilitated thousands of individuals in developing greater awareness, balance, and wholeness in their lives.

The most important thing to remember is to use creative visualization often, to make it a regular part of your life. Most people seem to find that it works best to practice it at least a little every day, especially when they are first learning.

In her books, Shakti suggests you have a regular creative visualization <u>meditation</u> period of fifteen minutes or so each morning when waking up, and each evening before sleeping (these are the times when it is most effective), as well as the middle of the day if you so desire. Always start your meditation periods with deep relaxation, then follow with any visualizations or affirmations you wish.

There are many different ways that creative visualization can be used, and it's up to you to remember to try them at appropriate times. Conscious, creative visualization may mean a new way of thinking and a new way of living. As such, it will take some practice.

Try it out in different situations and under different circumstances, and use it as often as you can for any type of problem solving. If you find yourself worried or puzzled about anything, or feeling discouraged or frustrated about a problem, ask yourself if there is a way you could use creative visualization to help you. Form a creative habit of using it at every appropriate moment.

Remember that most of us have years of negative thought patterns to overcome. It takes time to change some of these lifelong habits. And many of us have some underlying feelings and attitudes that can slow us down in our efforts to live more consciously.

Fortunately, creative visualization is such an innately powerful process that even five minutes of conscious, positive meditation can balance out hours, days, even years of negative patterns.

SIX-SECOND QUIETING REFLEX

The six-second quieting reflex was developed by Charles Stroebel, MD, PhD. His book can be hard to find and quite expensive. Here is a fairly brief introduction to Dr. Stroebel's technique drawn from his book.

"The Quieting Reflex is designed to counter the STRESS ALARM Reflex in which as many as 1700 physiological reactions occur in 6 seconds in a big stress situation. We usually experience the Fight or Flight side of this, in which we orient or turn our head toward the perceived stress, tense our jaw, forehead, eyes, belly, arms, and other muscles. We hold our breath or breathe fast and up in our chest. In 1-2 seconds, we get the adrenaline hit, heart rate initially slows, then speeds if we perceive danger, we perspire, hands and feet chill, and our bowels and bladder shut down. We have lots of energy with which to then run or fight even though most of our daily stresses are not life threats so it is usually inappropriate to fight or run. If we don't release this energy appropriately, we get exhausted and risk burnout, anger or anxiety. Some people instead go into a Freeze response and have to go to the bathroom immediately, or might get pale, dizzy, swoon or pass out as their heart rate drops. This is a shutdown response that typically comes when someone feels overwhelmed. Depression could follow."

Train yourself to have a six-second quieting reflex to counter the escalation of stress. This may take some practice and some repetition to make it a habit. Start with step 1. After this is practiced, when you first start to feel stress, your body will automatically go into steps 2 through 6 in releasing the stress physiology without you having to think about it.

Steps of the Six-second Quieting Reflex (from Dr. Stroebel's book)

> **STEP 1**: Notice what is bothering you. Purposely think of a recent stress event and tighten up like you normally do with stress (push tongue up, tighten jaw, forehead, shoulders, belly, and maybe arms) but only for about 2 seconds. (This simulates and starts the stress response.) Then go to step 2 to keep it from progressing.

> **STEP 2**: Smile <u>inwardly</u> with at least your mouth and eyes. Think of something heartwarming or amusing. (The smile starts triggering endorphin release so counters the stress chemistry.)

STEP 3: Now think of something like "Alert Mind, Calm Body," or "Everything Is Going To Be All right" (any mantra is good). This counter our negative stress reactions which actually stimulate more stress physiology.

STEP 4: Take a nice easy breath in (nose), during or after step 2 & 3.

STEP 5: As your breath goes back out (nose), relax your forehead, eyes, jaw, tongue, shoulders and belly, and let a wave of warmth and relaxation flow down through your body to your hands and feet, like the spreading warmth you feel after drinking some hot tea or soup. Warm hands are a sign of being more relaxed and at ease.)

STEP 6: Return to normal activity.

All of these steps are done Eyes Open, and it only takes 6 seconds total. Practice at stop lights, in waiting rooms, before answering phones, or when walking through doors. Choose the long line at the grocery store on purpose to practice and notice the results. This is such a subtle activity that no one will notice you doing it. Use reminder dots (on computer, dashboard, phone, mirror, clicker) or sticky notes, watch chimes, pop up screens, an unusual object like new desk item or mug to catch your attention. Use any or all of these so you can remember to take 6 seconds to practice the QR until it becomes an automatic behavior, a Quieting Reflex that keeps stress from escalating. Then you will have the habit and use it when needed.

The six-second quieting reflex is designed for you to find tranquility *within yourself*—not elsewhere.

LARGE MUSCLE ACTIVITY (LMA)

Our bodies are designed to do many marvelous things. Another quick way to reduce the immediate physiological effects of critical stress attacks is LMA. LMA stands for large muscle activity. If at all possible, try and grab a bit of time to walk (not saunter) somewhere for about five to fifteen minutes. This will use our largest muscles and have very positive influence on our bodies. Of course, you should allow and use positive and calming thoughts during this walk.

BENEFITS OF MUSIC

Research shows that music has positive effects on our psyche. Music has the ability to induce a calming effect on the brain. Stress, anxiety, or crisis can reduce brain activity and reduce the brain's ability to plan and execute. Lack of serotonin, a transmitter, may result in a depressed frame of mind.

Music can easily render a relaxing calm. It calms the body nerves and soothes the mind. Carefully chosen musical selections can induce sleep.

Everyone should have a different time, locale, and music selection to execute this strategy. Personalization is your cue. Find a simple locale to relax in and actually listen to the music.

When Mozart was composing at the end of the eighteenth century, the city of Vienna was so quiet that fire alarms could be given verbally by a shouting watchman mounted on top of St. Stefan's Cathedral. In twenty-first century society, the noise and activity levels are so high that it keeps knocking our bodies out of tune and out of their natural rhythms.

The effects music can have on your mind or brain depend largely on the kind of music you choose to listen to. Experience positive psychological effects of music by listening to only good music. Any melody pleasing to you is the sound that has the power of creating a calm. That's the joy and magic of music. Listening to music should deliver a relaxed and divine pleasure.

SIMPLIFY

This ever-increasing assault of sound and activity upon our ears, minds, and bodies adds to the stress load of civilized beings trying to live in extremely complex environments. Our brain, including all of its memories, hasn't kept up with rapidly increasing demands of daily living additionally fed by rapidly increasing technology. Basically, our brain is constantly and subconsciously doing its best trying to make us simplify.

Professional relaxation is a wonderful and effective way to clarify and disentangle our lives. Do it and you will get miraculous results!

> *"Each moment of worry, anxiety or stress represents lack of faith in miracles, for they never cease."* — *T.F. Hodge*

LAUGH

Laughter is just a marvelous medicine. Laughing can approach proper diet and exercise when it comes to keeping you healthy and disease free. Dr. Lee Berk, an associate professor at Loma Linda University in California says, "Laughter shuts down the release of stress hormones like cortisol. It also activates the production of feel-good neurochemicals like dopamine, which cause all sorts of calming, anti-anxiety benefits. Think of laughter as the yin to stress's yang." Dr. Berk has spent nearly three decades studying the ways the aftershocks of a good laugh ripple through your brain and body.

Even though you're about thirty times more likely to laugh around other people than when you are by yourself, laughter is surely beneficial for lowering levels of anxiety and reactions to stressful moments. The effects of humor and laughter on our physical and mental well-being are proven and extremely beneficial. A good laugh decreases levels of stress hormones like cortisol and adrenal, causes endorphin levels to rise, and strengthens our immune system. Laughter may also lessen pain. Isn't it funny that doing something silly is good for you?

While I'm not yet ready to think of laughter as a complete panacea, I can't disagree with the benefits associated with a lusty laughter. This is because laughing and humor helps you take things more lightheartedly and joyfully, breaking out of the stress-producing thoughts, increasing your sense of satisfaction, and going about your life more meaningful. It likewise assists you in connecting with others around you. It is not strange that people will find you more complete and likable.

FOUR: EXERCISE

Exercise is the second strategy of the R.**E**.A.D.Y. acronym.

> *"At times of great stress it is especially necessary to achieve a complete freeing of the muscles." - Konstantin Stanislavsky*

A recent scientific American study indicates a strong, healthy body results in a strong healthy mind. On that point, there is much scientific data showing similar outcomes—but that's the essence.

Exercise is *very important* to your overall wellness. You will be much better at managing anxiety, stress, scary thoughts, depression, tiredness, self-esteem; well, just about everything, if you are motivated to start and maintain an exercise program. The key is simplicity! The results are great!

This chapter deals only with physical exercise. Exercise is often equated with sports. However, medical research has discovered and produced research proving that physical exercise has definite health benefits and in some cases can improve our mental outlook as well as being an effective medication for preventing and treating certain diseases.

It is true any exercise is better than no activity. It is also true the best results can be obtained by selecting the right exercises for you. Doing any exercise and managing it for the correct duration of time at the proper volume and frequency will measurably help your physical and mental wellness.

A fitness program is one of the best things you can do. Physical activity can bring down your risk of chronic disease, improve your equilibrium and coordination, help you lose weight, improve your sleep habits, and increase your self-esteem.

It will take discipline and time management to develop your personal plan and strategy concerning exercise.

Consider the following proposition as a means to look at the many excellent professional plans which abound in books and on the Web. It is just important to get started.

Assessment: Assess your fitness; aerobic and muscular. Consult with your doctor next check-up. Flexibility and body composition (Body Mass Index) are important assessments. For certain, you will be well advised to do activities you most love. What are they? Are you going to choose between driving a bike, dancing, swimming, walking, running, or jumping rope? Why not make several of them part of your exercise plan?

Fitness Program Design: You'll need a well-defined plan in writing! Plan your fitness program by keeping in mind the good ideas you have found. Do you need to lose weight? Do you need overall physical well-being? Goals are important before you can gauge progress. You may desire to aim for at least one hundred and fifty minutes of moderate intensity aerobic activity—or seventy-five minutes of vigorous aerobic activity a week. Perhaps you will include two or more days of strength training a week.

Plan to do some kind of exercise every day. It can be a challenge at first. Make it easy; schedule exercise as you would any other appointment.

> *"You should not try to avoid stress any more than you would shun food, love or exercise." - Hans Selye*

Including cross-training of several types can keep exercise boredom at bay. By cross-training you might cut your chances of injuring or overusing one specific muscle or joint. Be adaptable and clever. Your best workout routines might include various activities, such as walking, bicycling, rowing, swimming, and strength training. As a by-product, you will develop different parts of your body.

Many people take up working out with frenzied zeal—working out excessively long or too intensely—and give up when their muscles and joints get sore or hurt. Plan time between sessions for your body to rest and recover. Remember, you are even trying to enjoy this!

Assemble Equipment: Quality athletic shoes need to be obtained. You can also experience various types of equipment at fitness centers. You may desire to join a fitness center. You can also use your imagination: make weights by filling old socks with beans or pennies or by partially filling a half-gallon milk jug with water or sand.

Start Action Plan: Be aware of the following as you begin your exercise plan:

- Start out slowly and gradually build up your speed.
- Consulting with and informing your doctor is a solid idea.
- Take plenty of time to warm up and cool down—easy walking or gentle stretching.
- Go at a pace you can continue for five to ten minutes without getting overly bored. Working slowly up to thirty to sixty minutes of exercise is your target. Fifteen minutes of exercise a couple of times a day may fit into your schedule better than a single thirty-minute session.
- Just remember to listen to your body. If you feel pain, shortness of breath, dizziness or nausea, call for a time out.
- Remember to be flexible and creative. If you're not feeling good, give yourself permission to take a day or two off.

Monitor Progress: Occasionally retake your personal fitness assessment. If you lose motivation, set new goals or try a new activity. Working out with a friend or taking a class at a fitness center may help too. You are, after all, trying to remain moving.

Here are some immediate ideas of where to start:

Cardiovascular Exercises:

Walking: Walking is the simplest, cheapest, and most comfortable sort of cardiovascular practice. It is the best starting point for anyone who is just starting to exercise. It is very low impact and is exceedingly convenient. Start slow, then gradually work up to walking longer and quicker. Finding a walking partner can help keep you motivated.

Jogging/Running: This is a stride up from walking. It is harder and puts more impact and stress on the body. If you are just starting an exercise program, work through fast walking before moving up to jogging.

Cycling: Riding a bike is an excellent non-impact form of cardio. Be trusted to abide by the conventions of the road and *always* wear a helmet.

Swimming: Swimming involves all the major muscles of the body. It is non-impact and is very useful for injury recovery. The major drawback is that you must know how to swim.

Exercise Club: There are many excellent facilities abound: YMCA, Curves, etc. The additional benefit of making friends and sustaining motivation are also important. You may also consider a personal trainer.

WebMD's 10 tips for making fitness a habit in your life.

1. Do a variety of activities you enjoy. Cross-train!
2. Commit to another person. Team up with others.
3. Make exercising a priority. Why not start now?
4. Exercise first thing in the morning before breakfast.
5. Or work out on your way home from work.
6. Exercise, even when you're "too tired".
7. Log your physical activity each week. Just write it down.
8. Be mindful of all the indicators of progress. Feel better now?
9. Walk—with a pedometer (or a dog).

Part of your exercise plan should include rewards. Maybe you will get accolades from friends and family, so share your successes freely. You will personally gain many dividends in your life. Enjoy! This is a great dividend!

If you already exercise regularly (twenty minutes three times a week at 75 percent of heart target rate), keep up the good work. If you don't work out regularly, it is never too late to get moving!

If you are just beginning aerobic activity you should know your target rate. You may figure target rate under the following method: subtract your age from 220; multiply times 75percent. This is the heart rate you want to work up to and maintain for twenty minutes three times a week. (five minutes warm-up – twenty minutes at target rate – five minutes cool-down)

The benefits of a regular exercise program are many and rewarding! Never forget the basic motivation to do this is: a strong healthy body results in a strong healthy mind. Why wouldn't you want to be more chipper, full of life, and bushy-tailed? My goodness, you might actually enjoy this.

FIVE: ATTITUDE

Attitude is the third strategy of the R.E.**A**.D.Y. acronym.

> *"Adopting the right attitude can convert a negative stress into a positive one"* – *Hans Selye*
>
> Dr. Selye held three doctorates (MD, PhD, DSc) and was forty-three times a Doctor Honoris Causa. Selye wrote some thirty-nine books and more than 1,700 articles on stress and related problems. He was nominated for the Nobel Prize ten times.

It is very important to understand that words used either silently to yourself or verbalized to others have meaning. Words mirror our attitude. Hans Selye was absolutely right. We must adopt (utilize or embrace) beneficial attitudes in our thinking and our external performance.

Just as it is said, "You are what you eat," the following saying is also true, "You are what you think." Your attitude could be detrimental due to making automatic or habitually wrong choices. We can choose otherwise!

When you are in control of your life, you can control the way in which you think (attitude). Work this the other way around. When you control what you think, you can control your life. Remember the dictum by Peter G. Hanson, MD: "Learn to ignore what you can't control. Learn to control what you can."

Attitude is all about mental outlook. Choices.

We have learned that much of our mental outlook is due to conscious or subconscious choices. There is an excellent quote by Dr. Kathleen Hall, "In every single thing you do, you are choosing a direction. Your life is a product of choices."

Negative attitudes habitually and deliberately proclaimed by you can have a surprisingly negative reaction from people when they respond to you. Their feedback can generate unfavorable strengthening of the negative thoughts within you. Your reaction might then be, "What have I done to deserve to be treated this way?"

How to deal with difficult people and situations will be the focus of this guide's Part Seven Yield strategy. Consequently, in this chapter the attitudes you have remain solely your personal adventure to control. You can select appropriate and positive attitudes. Yes, you can. That is called change. You can switch, change, or swap any reaction or thought (attitude) you have. You may have a strong and longtime negative attitude habit to overcome.

Learn to welcome change.

If you do not change, it is likely you will continue old, well used, and automatic attitudes. People who welcome change exploit new opportunities opening up on a constant basis. Success toward your long-term goals depends on adaptation, anticipation, or creation of change. Author Paul Pearsall has said, "All we accomplish or fail to accomplish is the direct result of our being in control of our thoughts."

Can we think ourselves healthy?

Yes, we can. "There is no longer any question that there is a link between the immune system and the brain," says Paul Pearsall in his book titled *Super Immunity: Master Your Emotions and Improve Your Health*. Every thought, every feeling is accompanied by a shower of neurochemicals as if it is a trip to our internal pharmacy.

Emotions can directly affect our health. This mind-body concept has been part of some Eastern and Western thought for centuries.

Here are detailed just a few suggestions to follow. They are easy. They will give you guidance as to how to direct your thoughts. Perhaps you can conjure some others. These will fit well into your life as an consequence, result, and effect.

- **Laugh**: There is no question that laughter is good for you. The presence of humor is one of the strongest predictors of mental acuity. Collect and tell jokes that are funny to you! Laughing is easy and uses less muscles that you can imagine.
- **Have love in your life**: Put as much thought into making your relationships work as you put into your job. Close ties with people (lovers, family, and friends) enhance life's good times and buffer the bad. You can also love a hobby.
- **Simplify everything**: The simpler your life, the more enhanced is your immune system. Things get so complex we lose the flow of living. The number of decisions you have to make during the day can exceed that of our ancestors and our own limits by the hundreds. The old bug-a-boo of time management is also part of this concept.
- **Accept sickness**: It is part of life. However, a positive attitude may lessen the length and severity of illness. Also, the more you work on your wellness, the less you will be sick.
- **See a doctor**: If you are sick or in pain, see a doctor. Use them as your employee and don't abandon your own responsibility. Do not wait!
- **Practice optimism**: It is better known as preventative medicine. Happiness, trust, and calmness are certainly worth attention.
- **Care for yourself first**: When you are upset or under high stress levels, or feel vulnerable, make yourself unwind. Practice your relaxation strategies. Exercise and diet are certainly also worthy of your attention.
- **Talk positively to yourself**: Good thoughts, positive thoughts, drive out the negative anxiety producing thoughts. Everything is going to be okay if you can say it to yourself—nicely. Be able to celebrate being alive. Why put up with anxiety?

- **Question your priorities and goals**: Is your life being led from within or from the expectations of others?

The following statement by Charles Swindoll sums up attitude very well: "The longer I live, the more I realize the impact of attitude on life. Attitude, to me, is more important than facts. It is more important than the past, than education, than money, than circumstances, than failures, than successes, than what others think or say or do."

Swindoll continues, "It is more important than appearance, giftedness or skill. It will make or break a company . . . a church . . . a home. The remarkable thing is we have a choice everyday regarding the attitude we will embrace for that day. The only thing we can do is play on the one string we have, and that is our attitude. I am convinced that life is 10 percent what happens to me and 90 percent how I react to it."

> *"The greatest weapon against stress is our ability to choose one thought over another." - William James*

SIX: DIET

Diet is the fourth strategy of the R.E.A.**D**.Y. acronym.

> *"To eat is a necessity, but to eat intelligently is an art."*
> — *François de La Rochefoucauld*

That quote is right to the point. It is a constant dilemma learning how to eat intelligently. There are absolutely loads of diet information available via books and online. For example: Google the word "diet" and get 134 million sites. Any good bookstore will have ten to twenty feet of diet books. You do not have the time to go through this mountain of information. Nevertheless, we can assume your motivation to eat correctly is quite high. You can easily research a good diet without much effort—properly motivated. Diet is best regarded as a word that describes *what* you eat, not so much *how much*!

There are two reasons to eat intelligently. One is physical health. The other is mental health. This is especially true concerning how you deal with stress. Your search for a plan revolves around finding a diet which meets both needs.

The best diet begins with the best medical advice you can get. The simplest strategy is to go online to get access to the Mayo Clinic Diet. It is a good place to start as it is constructed for your physical well-being. It also contains advice on food that is good for your mental well-being. It can certainly be adapted to your requirements.

Regimen and nutritional value are the key words to remember. *What* you eat and *when* you eat are central to your total wellness. Diet is not about abstinence from foods you may like but about when, where, and how much you eat. Additionally, eating certain foods might accelerate your distress levels.

As you go through the thought process in deciding how to adapt eating habits it would be good for you to do so with the hints discussed below.

Short list of the various foods to avoid:

Fried foods: They're difficult to digest and not very nutritious. Eating large quantities of fried foods only helps to increase your anxiety levels.

Dairy products: Butter, milk, and creams are beneficial in moderate amounts. Large quantities can easily exaggerate <u>adrenaline levels</u> increasing your anxious state.

Sugary foods: Candy, syrups, honeys, and chocolates seem like stress-relievers for those with a sweet tooth, but if you're suffering from distress these foods will only add to your quandary. They give you a temporary high from a <u>sugar rush</u>. Beware—the resulting crash can leave you depressed, melancholic, and anxious. Use and eat in moderation.

Acid forming foods: Yogurt, pickles, eggs, and sour cream (including the dairy and fried foods mentioned earlier) lessen the magnesium levels in your body; the result makes you feel tense and edgy.

Caffeine: Whether it's in coffee, energy drinks, or carbonated sodas, caffeine is one of the major ingredients to avoid weakening your ability to cope well. Caffeine naturally boosts your blood pressure and causes heart palpitation. Since caffeine gives you a boost of energy, a powerful restlessness or need to burn this energy off creates problems for you. Poor coping can result from too much caffeine inhibiting the chemicals that cause us to calm down. So have your coffee. Just drink it in moderation. Be alert!

Alcohol: Medical specialists have always recommended that alcohol should only be taken in moderation. This should be even more apparent for those suffering from anxiety or panic disorders. Mayo Clinic wisely advises two glasses of wine (or equivalent) is alright—more is not wise. Unfortunately, it's normal for sufferers of stress to turn to alcohol in an attempt to "escape". Unfortunately, the chance for alcohol dependency coupled with its potentially destructive characteristics make alcohol a potentially deadly concoction when mixed with anxiety.

A short list that includes food to eat:

There is good news. Wonderfully, there are countless numbers of great tasting meals keeping your anxiety at bay.

Fresh fruit: All fruits are delicious and nutritious. They are great when you need to eat something on the go with little to no preparation. Lots of fruits have detoxifiers that help you get rid of various chemicals that keep you tense and anxious. On top of that, they are packed with fiber and vitamins to keep you healthy and raring to go. Don't forget that eating a banana will almost immediately lower stress.

Water: This seems like a no-brainer. We forget how important H2O is in our lives. Constant hydration is very important in keeping your body flushed of toxins and reenergized. Drinking water is not the same as drinking your favorite sweetened and carbonated beverages. Stick to the real thing and you'll be the better for it.

Tryptophan rich foods: Turkey, chicken, oats and soy contain amino acids that help you relax while boosting your metabolism and sleep patterns. Tryptophan is a precursor to the chemical serotonin which helps calm your mind even during the most stressful moment.

Omega-3 fatty acids: Walnuts, flax seeds, and seafood such as salmon and shrimp go a long way in alleviating stress and reducing anxiety. Researchers have reported that people who feel depressed and stressed are usually lacking these nutrients.

Complex carbohydrates: One particular group of nutrients that will help you curb your anxiety are complex carbohydrates. Complex carbohydrates include foods, such as potatoes, pasta, cereal, rice, nuts, and corn. Bear in mind, however, that complex carbohydrates are particularly unhealthy for those prone to or who suffer from diabetes. Since complex carbohydrates are designed to raise your blood sugar level, these foods are not recommended for those who need to keep their blood sugar low and regulated.

Vegetables: Vegetables really are good for you. Just like fruits, vegetables are high in nutrition while being able to deliver quite a wallop in terms of fiber. This helps you detoxify your body and can keep the chemicals in your body clean and balanced. On top of that, foods such as tofu, whole grain meals, and black beans can act as a powerful muscle relaxant that helps you feel energized yet calm at the same time. Native Americans ate the three sisters comprised of corn, beans and squash which automatically gave them excellent protein.

Remember, keeping your diet in check may seem harder than it looks, but getting rid of your anxiety producing diet should be your first step to an anxiety free life. A good diet is a lot easier than you think. It is strategy; what you buy makes a difference. You eat what you buy!

There are certain suggestions worth trying: Eat at the same time during the day if possible; do not eat in your workspace; eat 'down' by enjoying a good breakfast and a lighter healthy lunch; and eat a light, well-balanced dinner. When you eat at home try to mimic fine dining which includes kitchen service (portion control) and avoids 'family service heaping platters' except for holidays. Oh, and have some music on rather than television.

SEVEN: YIELD

Yield is the fifth strategy of the R.E.A.D.**Y**. acronym.

> *"There is no greater misfortune than underestimating your enemy.*
> *Underestimating your enemy means thinking they are evil.*
> *Thus you destroy your three treasures **
> *and become an enemy yourself.*
> *When two great forces oppose each other, the victory will go*
> *to the one that knows how to yield."*
> — *Lao Tzu, Tao Te Ching * Simplicity, patience, compassion.*

Yield is the only part of your wellness acronym strategy that focuses directly on how *you* can deal with other people who have a distress-producing effect upon you and your goals. Direct contact with a stranger, partner, colleague, assistant, or boss can frustrate, hinder, or obstruct progress towards your goals. These transactions are able to perform an amazing number of things which can give you bad feelings and possible distress. However, your adaptation (i.e. yielding) to a particular distress producing transaction can easily return a great and positive feeling. This will lead to healthy coping.

How is it possible? Words have meaning. Yield has many negative descriptions and connotations. However, we react almost unthinkingly to yellow yield traffic signs which simply mean "Go ahead with care and don't crash into another car." Learning to yield is a good attribute. Continuing to "bump into walls" is a bad attribute.

The seeds of adaptation, innovation, and confidence are always within us; sometimes it takes a crisis to nourish and encourage their growth.

In a stress crisis you should pursue simplicity, patience, and compassion: these three are your greatest treasures, your blessings. Try to be simple in actions and thoughts. Be innovative and patient with both friends and enemies. Above all else, be compassionate toward yourself.

"Keep your friends close, and your enemies closer," is a saying by Sun-Tzu uttered 400 years BC. Think about it! What does "closer" mean?

You can learn a lot from people you dislike. Truthfully, you may even understand your enemies better than your friends. There are plenty of times when such a person can actually help to better your thinking and position on an issue.

In this chapter you are being asked to understand and accept the positive aspects of the word "yield". What do a few examples of this approach mean to you—can you use them positively? A good mantra for you would be: You reap what you sow—you yield (harvest) what you plant. All you need to do is supply the processes necessary to generate and encourage the return most supportive of you and your over-arching goals.

When confronted by another person who communicates to you in a stress-raising manner, train your brain to create and forge a reply "blueprint." Most people cannot do this 'on their feet' at the moment of confrontation. Whether you are like this or not, try my acronym device of the T.O.P.S. Plan (no—it does not mean take off pounds sensibly):

> **T** = Think. Buy time necessary to take the time to think! There is absolutely nothing wrong with being positive at this point. The last thing you need is an argument—you might not be adept at it. You don't need all that much time. It is important to get some time by yourself. That is not fleeing—it is responding positively. However, you're advised to get out of the spotlight long enough to work out a sensible response. Your response is a great way to work your goals and consider your opportunity to do so. A sample response could be, "What a great idea!" (Maybe it is not—but don't say that!) "I'll need to research this. Let me get back to you." (Set a time.)

O = Opportunity. During this think time—you can certainly be turning situations in your favor by featuring them as opportunities for you. What can you communicate in order to achieve that? This could be a chance to attain your goals.

P = Plan. Your aspirations can now turn into actions. Your thoughts can now be put to paper; you can start constituting your action plan. Words do have meaning. This is true for you as well as to whom you are communicating. Choose your words with care. This is precisely why you are putting them down on paper! Make sure your plan can be supervised! When you are satisfied, this plan can then be given to the person relaying the stress. Make sure that if you bargained with, "What a great idea. Let me work on that and get back to you at 3 p.m." Make sure you do so!

S = Supervise. A large percentage of time your plan will be accepted and possibly improved. Now all you have to do is supervise the approved plan!

One thing to consider when you are on the T = Think step is to ask the question, "Is this a healthy human relationship?" You are analyzing the transaction which just happened. Was it:

- Completely rational?
- Irrational?
- Some of both?

Basically, you are observing for yourself whether there is a game being played. Do they know it? Maybe they do not. Many games are most intensely played by disturbed people; the more disturbed they are, the harder they play.

Your life can be filled with dreams and fantasies shared with no one. Your work can be filled with processes and procedures that do not include anyone. No doubt you will be involved with rituals which include others but have no consequences. A good example of this would be a common conversation starter, "Good morning, how are you? Nice day, huh?" During the day you will have social pastimes with others—maybe talking about their new car, children, trips, and so on. However, now you are stuck in a transaction in which you feel something is wrong—so wrong you get "distressed."

Look for a possible 'game.' Games are clearly different from dreams, processes, rituals and pastime. A game's two chief characteristics are: (1) their ulterior motives, and; (2) the payoff.

Let's analyze some basic and simple transactional games defined by Eric Berne in his book, *Games People Play* (there are many more):

- Debtor: "You owe me!"
- Why Does This Always Happen to Me: "You must be at fault!"
- Now I've Got You, You Son-of-a-Bitch!: "I knew you would fail!"
- See What You Made Me Do!: "You got in my way!"
- Ain't It Awful?: "You must be the problem!"
- If It Weren't For You!: "Things would go so much smoother."
- Look How Hard I've Tried!: "I sure do wish you would try harder!"
- Uproar: "I can leave and slam the door—you tick me off!"
- I'm Only Trying To Help You!: "Too bad you're not doing a good job."
- If I Told You Once I've Told You Hundreds of Times!: "Not again!"

When you get into situations and transactions where you feel or can identify that a game is being played – this is a good time to buy some time and use the T.O.P.S. plan.

An excellent plan (T.O.P.S. or not) is one which avoids disagreement and/or ignorance. How can this happen?

Successful plans will focus on:

- Never sound disagreeable—there is nothing wrong with, "What a great idea, but I feel *we* can improve it . . . I'll get back to you." (You are buying time to think!)
- Never sound ignorant—research and bring yourself up to speed with the facts.

- Always participate in the agreed upon solution(s)—one of which is probably now due to your input
- Always be patient, plain, and appear understanding
- Always keep the communication clear and "in time with" the other person. "In time with" is a classical interpretation in the usage of the word intimacy.

Many wonder about negative versus positive thinking. Which way do you want to go? Understanding the negatives of any situation can easily lead to some very positive results. The challenge is to state the problem in a way that will allow a solution.

The worst case scenario could always be included. The goal is an agreeable plan. Not is it good or bad (the situation or the plan)? You will notice that the keywords here are *agreeably plan*. So why be disagreeable getting it formulated?

It would be well for you to crown your yielding response by depicting a competent plan which features effectiveness. This effectiveness is often illustrated by the notion of commercial viability. Commercial viability is defined by adhering to and satisfying three spheres: (1) money (budget); (2) time (schedule), and; (3) quality (viability). Your plan must cope with these three things in an inventive, thorough, and clear fashion. For example, to achieve the highest quality you may have to negotiate more money in the budget or more time in the schedule or both. Don't be afraid to be effective!

A successful professional has been using the following statement with great success when formulating plans, "Would you rather be right or would you rather be *effective*?"

President John F. Kennedy speaking in support of the plan to go to the moon stated, "We choose to go . . . not because [it is] easy, but because [it is] hard, because that goal will serve to measure and organize the best of our energies and skills, because that challenge is one that we are willing to accept, one we are unwilling to postpone, and one which we intend to win."

Always keep in mind the analogy which depicts water as the great symbol for yielding. Water yields to whatever it hits. However, by using persistence, patience, and simplicity, it wins—through erosion. Don't forget that persistence, patience, and compassion are your treasures! Simplicity is your objective.

Finally, when learning to use the yield strategy, never forget Dr. Hansen's mantra of stress control: Learn to control what you can, and learn to ignore what you can't control.

> *"If you think you are beaten, you are;*
> *if you think you dare not, you don't.*
> *If you'd like to win, but think you can't,*
> *It's almost a cinch you won't,*
> *If you think you'll lose, you've lost.*
> *For out in the world we find*
> *Success being with a fellow's will:*
> *It's all in the state of mind.*
>
> *If you think you're outclassed, you are.*
> *You've got to think high to rise.*
> *You've got to be sure of yourself before*
> *you can ever win a prize.*
> *Life's battles don't always go*
> *To the stronger or faster man,*
> *But sooner or later the man who wins*
> *Is the one who thinks he can."*
> *— Walter D. Wintle*

EIGHT: P.O.W.E.R. OVERVIEW

> *"Competence, like truth, beauty, and contact lenses, is in the eye of the beholder." - Laurence J. Peter*

Competence. That expressive word is a major result of the strategies in the P.O.W.E.R. acronym. Competent people automatically have power and seemingly automatically employ the skills of these acronyms. Their behavior is fundamentally competent, effective, and capable. Others trust their competence. They also joyously cope with stress. They enjoy it!

You also may develop competence and trust as lifelong goals. Those are superb objectives. You can use the strategies in the P.O.W.E.R. acronym in order to increase competence and trust and make these qualities fundamentally automatic.

- **P** stands for **persistence**. You will discover this means tenacity, firmness, and steadfastness toward your goals.
- **O** stands for **opportunity**. This will help you find good fortune and favorable circumstances. It is work—but you can create your own opportunities.
- **W** stands for **wellness**. Basically, you should be sound and whole mentally and physically in order to thrive doing the full acronym. For the P.O.W.E.R. acronym to perform at the maximum, **W** (wellness) needs to be a central dynamic force and maintained—this means you have prepared, maintained, and become R.E.A.D.Y.!
- **E** stands for **energy**. You'll need strategies designed to show others that you have ardor, moxie, vitality, and zeal. Can you use

your strategies to accomplish satisfactory completion, which is defined as getting it done: (1) on time; (2) on budget, and; (3) with predicted quality? Be aware that total perfection will often lose and not be the answer. Effectiveness is much stronger that absolute perfection.

- **R** stands for **role**. You'll deal with quality and quantity of the routines, style, and conduct of various roles as you do your job, family relations, and social friends.

Competent people have the quality of demonstated ability. In every task you may face the need for the capacity to do something. What does this mean? In addition to abilities, you should be able to show the capacity to perform. Both qualities make up a competent person. Not only will you gain confidence, the P.O.W.E.R. acronym can also give you trust.

It is not true that you either have trust or you don't. Trust is a powerful asset created by you because it is tangible, practical, and logical. You can be wonderfully creative at becoming a trusted partner, friend, or colleague.

Trust is very basic to successful interpersonal relationships.

Here are a few hints to get you started:

Actually do what you say you'll do! A critically major process of building trust is to do what you say you will do. Follow through!

Honor all of your promises. Trust mandates the quality of dependability. If you cannot complete any promise you've made, you are obliged to explain face-to-face why you cannot honor your promise. If you must, make a new promise and fulfill it (knowing now that you can).

Tell the truth. It's decidedly simple to issue a little white lie. You may even be trying to protect someone. Tell the truth. Even if this is not very pleasant, you will become much more trustworthy.

Speak your feelings. If you only communicate hard facts, you may appear to be cold and distant. All people are emotional and rational beings. Life is about balancing both equally.

Keep secrets imparted to you. Never blab and never gossip. Enough said. You trust people who are discreet. If you reveal all, your confidant will cease to trust you.

Be neutral when placed in difficult predicaments. Don't choose sides until you're certain you have discovered and know all the hard facts.

Be competent. Go to lengths to display interpersonal skills and/or professional ability. You may have many skills. Why not put them on display?

Display loyalty. This refers to your ability to protect others, to be on the same side, both in their presence and (this is important) in their absence. Trust is present when a person knows they have loyalty from you. Always talk about someone as if they were there in the room.

NINE: PERSISTENCE

Persistence is the first strategy in the **P**.O.W.E.R. acronym.

> *"Persistence conquers all things." - Benjamin Franklin*

Persistence is the ability to maintain action, regardless of your quickly developed opinions and conclusions. You push on even when you feel like throwing in the towel. Persistence will ultimately provide its own motivation. If you continue taking effective action, you'll eventually get results, and results can be very motivating. For instance, you may feel a lot more enthusiasm about dieting and working via the R.E.A.D.Y. acronym once you've lost those first ten pounds and feel your clothes fitting more loosely.

Motivational speaker Og Mandino has stated, "If you persist long enough you will win." Another respected motivational speaker Lee Iacocca has said, "You've got to say, I think that if I keep working at this and want it badly enough I can have it. It is called persistence."

Persistence involves both effort and zeal. So how do you know when to press on, when to give up? Is your plan still correct? If not, update the plan. Is your goal still correct? If not, update or abandon your goal. There's no honor in sticking to a goal that no longer inspires you. It is best to be wise. Persistence is not stubbornness.

Victory comes to those who remain—with the most tenacity, strength, and resilience. Persistence is dogged determination. It leads to you having power. Persistence leads to the will to succeed. Keep in mind the old Buddhist saying, "In the confrontation between the stream and the rock, the stream always wins—not through strength, but through persistence."

Persistence has tremendous value. You cannot, however, stubbornly cling to the past. If you find yourself doing just that—you have already proven you are not good at persistence.

Other people's goals can be catalogued: analyzed by their actions. What have they done? What they do is really what they want to do.

If you can be super-clear about your goals, you'll accordingly be more persistent. Your growing consistency of action will produce consistency of outcomes. Persistence of vision leads to persistence of action. Persistence of action will produce consistency of results.

Persistent people begin their success where others end in failure.

At work, your boss is very difficult and demanding and hard to work with. One day, you find out the boss has been fired. If you want to be promoted into that line of work, you must be proactive and persistent. You work harder, make deadlines, stay focused, and do the best you can, and then some. Get the job that you deserve! You should be very happy and proud of yourself. You began your success where someone else wasn't doing their job and failed. They were fired, you got promoted.

Michelangelo once said, "Study the masters." In that vein, you can look at people who changed the world. These are well-known people who persisted and their lives are worth studying:

- Thomas Jefferson
- Martin Luther King
- Winston Churchill
- William Shakespeare
- Abraham Lincoln
- Christopher Columbus
- Aristotle
- Mother Teresa

Stephen Hawking defied a horrible disease for fifty years. Diagnosed with motor neurone disease at twenty-one, he was given two years to survive. He has not merely survived but prospered in a way few could rival. His positive outlook and persistence almost certainly has made a difference. Successful treatment requires extraordinary commitment, attention to detail, and a refusal to live with second best. Professor Hawking has had a successful treatment and a career, which required extraordinary commitment, attention to detail, refusal to accept second best, and persistence. His strategy, at its very basic level, was to overcome an ugly, fatal, and debilitating disease.

J.K Rowling, the author of *Harry Potter*, spoke to the graduating class of Harvard in June 2008. She didn't speak about success. She talked about her failures. "You might never fail on the scale I did," Rowling told that privileged audience. "But it is impossible to live without failing at something, unless you live so cautiously that you might as well not have lived at all—in which case, you fail by default." She should know, right? The author didn't magically become richer than the Queen of England overnight. Penniless, recently divorced, and bringing up a child on her own, she wrote the first Harry Potter book on an old manual typewriter. Twelve publishers rejected the manuscript! A year after, she was given the green light by Barry Cunningham from Bloomsbury, who agreed to publish the book, but insisted she get a day job because there was no money in children's books. What if she stopped at the first rejection? The fifth? Or the tenth? Persistence was the key.

TEN: OPPORTUNITY

Opportunity is the second strategy in the P.**O**.W.E.R. acronym.

> *"When written in Chinese, the word 'crisis' is composed of two characters. One represents danger and the other represents opportunity." - John F. Kennedy*

What is your greatest source of opportunity? People. Regardless of what your goals are, there is a person who can provide you with an opportunity. However, there is a yo-yo effect. It's odd that some of your best opportunities will be made available to you because you created or relayed an opportunity for another person. The cliché is "Pay it forward."

The self-image of yourself will play a role in the type of opportunities made available to you. You are a valuable asset, and if you present yourself as such, others will see your assets. Never come across as impaired or urgently desperate. Opportunities come to those who instill confidence. Shakespeare said, "All the world's a stage." Use it!

There is a high probability that there will be many events in your life and career which will provide opportunities to further your goals to your benefit. Some opportunities will just befall as good luck. You could train yourself to recognize and use them. Some opportunities will be possibilities you have created on purpose. You could enjoy and take advantage of them.

We can be so very blind to opportunity for many reasons. One reason is, you may not have a good daily awareness of the core goals you have acquired. This can make it difficult, if not impossible, to recognize opportunities right under your eyes. Good luck; new possibilities do reward those who are prepared to take it in.

Fresh opportunities are virtually impossible to create if you remain satisfied with things, or because of a shy or passive disposition. In order to recognize opportunities, or create them, you will have to first acknowledge you are going to have to do what needs to be done and take uncomfortable tasks of realization. Your comfort zone will need to be expanded to include these jobs. Good quotes abound on this thought. Winston Churchill said, "A pessimist sees the difficulty in every opportunity; an optimist sees the opportunity in every difficulty." Thomas Edison said, "The reason a lot of people do not recognize opportunity is because it usually goes around wearing overalls looking like hard work."

If opportunity only dances with those already on the dance floor, you are going to have to learn to dance. That is a metaphor for change. Change and opportunity go hand in hand.

Your greatest source of opportunity is people! Regardless of what kind of opportunity you are looking for, there is someone somewhere who is in a position to assist you. If you have a service to offer, there is someone who needs that help. If you have a product to sell, or an order to fill, it doesn't matter what that product is or what you need to fulfill your order; somewhere out there are buyers and sellers that can assist you.

It makes no difference what kind of opportunity you are seeking. Whether it is in the realm of products, services, guidance, assistance, or knowledge, you can find the right person or group of people. People represent your greatest source of opportunities. Obviously, you can read about or talk to successful people as well.

Your self-image will make a vast difference in the type of opportunities you attract to yourself. If you consider yourself as a valuable asset, and you submit yourself as such, others will view you that way as well. You never want to come across as needy or desperate. This is true whether you are looking for a job, a teammate, or a business collaborator. Self-confidence encourages people to have confidence in you. Opportunities come to those who instill confidence.

You can take steps to boost your self-confidence. The Mayo Clinic has identified four things about which to think in this respect:

1. **Identify troubling conditions or situations.** Think about the conditions or situations that seem to deflate your self-esteem. Common triggers might include: A business presentation or crisis at work or home. A challenge with a spouse, loved one, coworker or other close contact. A change in life circumstances, such as a job loss or a child leaving home.
2. **Become aware of thoughts and beliefs.** Once you've identified troubling conditions or situations, pay attention to your thoughts and attitudes about them.
3. **Challenge negative or inaccurate thinking.** Your initial thoughts might not be the only possible way to view a situation— so test the accuracy of your thoughts. Ask yourself whether your view is consistent with facts and logic or whether other explanations for the situation might be plausible.
4. **Adjust your thoughts and opinions.** Now replace negative or inaccurate thoughts with accurate, constructive thoughts.

Try these strategies:

- **Use hopeful statements.** Talk to yourself with kindness and encouragement. Pessimism can be a self-fulfilling prophecy. For instance, if you think your presentation isn't going to go well, you might indeed stumble through it. Try telling yourself things such as, "Even though it's tough, I can handle this situation."
- **Learn to forgive yourself.** Everyone makes mistakes—and mistakes aren't permanent reflections of you as a person. They're isolated moments in time. Tell yourself, "I made a mistake, but that doesn't make me a bad person."
- **Avoid 'should' and 'must' statements.** If you find that your thoughts are full of these words, you might be putting unreasonable demands on yourself or on others. Taking out these words from thoughts can lead to more realistic expectations.
- **Focus on the positives.** Think about the good parts of your life. Remind yourself of things that have gone well lately. Consider the skills you've used successfully to cope with challenging situations.

- **Refute upsetting thoughts.** You don't need to react negatively to negative thoughts. Instead, think of negative thoughts as signals to try new, healthy patterns. Ask yourself, "What can I think and do to make this less stressful?"
- **Encourage yourself toward success.** Give yourself credit for making positive changes. For example, "My presentation might not have been perfect, but my colleagues asked questions and remained engaged—which means that I accomplished my goal."

> *"I always tried to turn every disaster into an opportunity." - John D. Rockefeller*

Use any word you want to define opportunity. "Debacle" is a good one. Gosh, now that's an opportunity! You can grab the golden ring and succeed. What is the result of your good planning and work? You can have positive achievement!

ELEVEN: WELLNESS

Wellness is the third strategy in the P.O.**W**.E.R. acronym.

> *"To keep the body in good health is a duty, otherwise we shall not be able to keep our mind strong and clear." - Buddha*

Wellness is necessary for all aspects of the P.O.W.E.R. acronym to perform at their maximum influence on your goals. The development and maintenance of your wellness are cultivated by actively pursuing and fulfilling the R.E.A.D.Y. acronym.

It certainly makes sense not to be sick. It could be you are ailing, run down, laid up. It could be you are debilitated or hospitalized. It could be you have both mental and physical frailties.

Wonderfully, you could be strong, healthy, and well. This is the state of health you should be experiencing in order to seek and obtain all of your beneficial goals. Much has been written supporting research that long-term inadequate coping with stress has high rates of probability of getting sick. Distress will most certainly stonewall or slow your long-term goals.

To be in good health and using effective and healthy stress-coping strategies is central to the objectives of the acronym concepts used in this guide.

When instituting the wellness disciplines of **R**elaxation, **E**xercise, **A**ttitude, **D**iet, and **Y**ield you will find yourself successfully on the journey to greatly improved coping plus physical and mental health. How to activate wellness disciplines effectively in your life—this is totally up to you.

The purpose of this guidebook is to encourage simplicity, motivation, and discipline in your problem-solving process. This allows organization, enthusiasm, and proficiency so you could manage and enjoy your stress and life goals.

Wellness is a large partner in the process of gaining P.O.W.E.R.: It makes you R.E.A.D.Y.!

TWELVE: ENERGY

Energy is the fourth strategy in the P.O.W.**E**.R. acronym.

> *"Even if you are on the right track, you'll get run over if you just sit there." - Will Rogers*

This strategy focuses on impressions, recognition, and perceptions. Powerful people pursue their goals with energy, ardor, and zeal. The perception of you and your behavior should reflect such energy. You will appear to have stamina and strength. You will appear to have spirit and vigor. Those around you will perceive initiative and effectiveness. Being with you will be a positive experience.

Energy can be an effective implement in your new 'tool box' of strategies. You should analyze how people perceive the energy you emit. Positive or negative beliefs, emotions, and words radiate energy. You can go into a room feeling tension in the air, as opposed to a room which is upbeat and relaxed.

These days it's quite common knowledge that our attitude and state of mind directly affects our physical state. However, many people are constantly worried, stressed out, or just bored and unhappy. Others are always busy thinking about how tired they are. Having this kind of mindset can only help to make you and those around you tired and unmotivated.

Here are a few changes of mindset that you can start applying right now, to increase your physical and mental energy:

- **Act energetically!** You should _be energetic_ before you become energetic. Walk tall, speak out loud, and move about energetically. Do your best to never look tired. Soon your brain will start trusting your body! Don't be like Dagwood Bumstead and let anyone see you as lazy!
- **Take control of your energy level** Keep track of your physical and mental level of energy. Notice how it's affected by anything— what you eat or drink, your sleep and wake up time, places you go to, people you talk to, anything. Start to recognize and eliminate "energy wasters" from your life, like negative thinking and insignificant others that suck the life force out of you.
- **Set short term, challenging, yet achievable goals** Remind yourself every day why you're doing it, and be proud and happy for any small achievement along the way. When you fail, and you will, don't beat yourself up and don't give up. Keep on running toward your goals.
- **Think positive!** Negative thinking is one of the most common 'energy drainers'. You have to avoid it as much as you can. A favorite cliché is, "Always look on the bright side of life." It really only takes some practice. You can "train" yourself to think more positively. In any situation, try to find the positive side; be thankful; look closely and see how fortunate you are. Make a list! You will have obstacles; see them as challenges, and see failures and disappointments as lessons. It's about learning from them and moving on.
- **Eliminate (or ignore) 'energy drainers'** News is stressful. Get less of it. In general, filter information. You don't actually have to know about everybody else's problems. Certainly, you don't have to solve them! Every time someone gets on your nerves or hurts in you in some way, don't waste time thinking about it too much, dismiss it as something of the past as quickly as you can.
- **Take the next steps to becoming energetic** Having the right mindset is usually not enough to make you energetic. Sleep, nutrition, and physical activity are a few factors determining your energy level. It is a good thought if you see here the effectiveness of your R.E.A.D.Y. development!

Improving each one of those areas may take time and effort, and you'd probably have to make a few changes to your habits and your lifestyle. Remember to keep the proper mindset while working on changing your habits. However, don't put too much pressure on yourself. Take small steps and give yourself time to adjust. You may already know about a few things that you do (or don't do) that lowers the perception of your energy level. Asking trusted partners or colleagues about your energy level perceptions may give you some guidance.

Always use the following concept of effectiveness as your model!

Can you use your strategies to accomplish satisfactory completion— which is defined as getting it done to the best of your ability (viability): (1) on time; (2) on budget, and; (3) with predicted quality? Be aware that total perfection will often lose and not be the answer. Being able to predict and accomplish (1), (2), and (3) with viability and effectiveness is the answer!

Effectiveness is *always* much stronger than persuing absolute perfection. Why? The perfectionist has trouble meeting deadlines! Their managers and supervisors will say, "They do great work, but can't meet the timelines. Gotta fire them."

THIRTEEN: ROLE

Role is the fifth strategy in the P.O.W.E.**R.** acronym.

> *"I think once you're in the public eye, whether you're a boss, a teacher or whatever you do, that you're automatically in the position of role model. You have people looking up to you, so whether you choose to accept it or not is a different question." - Talib Kweli*

A major focus of the **R** acronym is perception, teamwork and flexibility. That simply means the ability to easily *change*. James A. Belasco and Ralph C. Stayer in their book *Flight of the Buffalo* said, "Change is hard because people overestimate the value of what they have—and underestimate the value of what they may gain by giving it up."

Are we talking about our personal life or jobs? Both and more. For example, instituting several changes might be needed to accomplish fulfilling your various roles and reaching your overarching goals. This flexibility to change can happen in your personal life as well as simultaneously in your profession.

Here's a quick list of a few areas that can be analyzed:

- Manner of conducting oneself: do you have social graces and ethics?
- The modus operandi of your day: do you practice time management?
- Management of your effectiveness: do you perform effectively?
- Presentation/style: do you sell your talent into the public eye?
- Control of what is done: do you have central and basic practices?
- If you think a problem is out there, that very thought is the problem.

People need to have confidence in your manner of conducting yourself to properly work toward your goals. The most significant aspect of this reliance is *competence*. Competence includes your character, capabilities, skills, results, and track record. All these measures are vital.

Different words may express the idea, but if you cut down the words to their essence, you'll end up with a wonderful balance of quality and competence. People will have confidence in you and your work.

Never say, "I was never quite sure what I was supposed to be doing." Always say, "These are the things I want to do—I have a plan!" The objective of the strategy to control your role is to gain direct discussion as to your goals: a healthy, truthful, and controlled discussion.

It is tricky to attempt to be a role model. In a recent study, a control group was asked what qualities they looked for in role models. They mentioned qualities like compassion, fearlessness, and listening skills. The most often mentioned attribute of a role model was their ability to inspire others.

Role models display a passion for their work and have the ability to pass on to others their passion. Role models illustrate publicly their values. People respect those who act in support of their beliefs. Role models are perceived as externally focused on others. They are not focused on themselves.

Maybe you should be aware that you are a person whose behavior might be imitated by others! It is entirely possible that you're involved in difficult situations or transactions as a result of (oh no!) being someone else's difficult person. It could be that you are certainly not a difficult person, just not coping very well, and their perception indicates you are difficult.

The very nature and contents of your job description should be studied for its clarity and relationship with your skills and life goals. How does it fit your skills? How does it advance your career? How does it lead to eventual success—both monetary and personal?

Attempt to have your job description fit you and your path to success: again, change and adapt. Control what you can!

> *"The truth is that stress doesn't come from your boss, your kids, your spouse, traffic jams, health challenges, or other circumstances. It comes from your thoughts about these circumstances."* - Andrew Bernstein

FOURTEEN: RESOURCES

Resources are literally everywhere. In addition to simplicity of approach, this guidebook is simple in mission to organize your thought and utilization processes. Organize your written records and you will find a normal place to file suggestions and information as it comes into your hands. Alternatively, you may find that just knowing how to classify information and where to put it in your brain will help you on your journey.

What follows are a few excellent ideas in which to start looking for further coverage of the aspects of R.E.A.D.Y. for P.O.W.E.R. Your searches may indeed be broader as you go. Choose wisely for yourself and good luck!

WARNING

Many people use Wikipedia to gather knowledge for many things, including health and stress matters. A new May 2014 study by authors of the Journal of the American Osteopathic Association has found that Wikipedia entries contradicted latest medical research 90 percent of the time.

Health care professionals, trainees, and patients should use caution when using Wikipedia to answer questions. Nine out of ten entries analyzed on the crowd-sourced encyclopedia contained assertions that were contradicted by the peer-reviewed sources. Only the entry on concussions escaped the review error-free.

The authors laid particular stress on medical professionals; a recent study found that 50 percent of physicians admitted using Wikipedia as a reference source.

RECOMMENDED WEBSITES:

Family Doctor: familydoctor.org Useful information on making healthy lifestyle choices; also a great site with accurate information concerning common illnesses.

Mayo Clinic: mayoclinic.com Easy to navigate and much medical information about various medical conditions; thorough diet information and stress discussions. Good choice.

Mayo Clinic Healthy Living: healthyliving.mayoclinic.org Excellent site which focuses on the wellness journey.

WebMD: webmd.com Much helpful information and a great general choice.

American Heart Association: ww.heart.org Stress affects each of us in different ways. The American Heart Association offers advice on how to deal with stress.

American Institute of Stress: www.stress.org/management-tips Just as stress is different for each of us, there is no stress reduction strategy that is a panacea.

Stress Management Resources from MindTools: www.mindtools.com/smpage.htm More than one hundred stress management tips and techniques, helping you manage the job-related stress in your life.

Shakti Gawain - free eBooks download: www.gobookee.org/creative-visualization-workbook-shakti-gawain/ The Relaxation & Stress Reduction Workbook.

Inner Health Studio: www.innerhealthstudio.com/stress-management-worksheets.html Stress management worksheets that will help you identify your causes of stress and find healthy coping skills to deal with stress. Great site.

Life Map Guide: www.babyzone.com Strangely titled site for a well-worked-out system of creating a life map. Not just for kids!

Relaxation Techniques: www.essenceofstressrelief.com Relaxation techniques helping turn on your body's own natural tranquilizer.

Energy Access Tools: http://energyandmotivation.com As they say, "Being energetic starts in your mind. If you want to become an energetic person, you have to start thinking like one."

Successful People Habits: www.briantracy.com Brian Tracy takes thirty years of experience and communicates how to create good habits.

Recognize Opportunity: http://advancedlifeskills.com What does opportunity look like?

Work-Related Stress: www.health.com As they say, "Specific work situations that are likely to make your blood boil."

Leadership: http://newdirectionsinmanagement.com Wonderful site for organization management led by F.G. (Sandy) Scott who authored this book's Foreword.

RECOMMENDED BOOKS:

The Relaxation & Stress Reduction Workbook, by Davis, Robbins, Eschelman, McKay, and Fanning. Recipes for relaxation. Easy to understand.

Don't Sweat the Small Stuff – And Its All Small Stuff, by Richard Carlson. This book will allow you to stop and 'smell the roses.'

The Relaxation Response, by Herbert Benson. This is a groundbreaker for development of the mind-body movement.

Stress Free For Good: 10 scientifically proven life skills for health and happiness, by Luskin and Pelletier. This book makes it clear that practice, practice, and practice is the "secret."

Coping With Stress: Effective People and Processes, by C. R. Snyder. Self Confidence: O.K. what problem is next? I'm ready coach, send me in!

Five Good Minutes: 100 Morning Practices to Help You Stay Calm and Focused All Day Long, by Jeffrey Brantley. You don't have to use them all. Find your perfect fit. Experiment!

What Next?: The Millennial's Guide to Surviving and Thriving in the Real World, by Michael Price. A good read, even for those who are not Millennial.

Margin: Restoring Emotional, Physical, Financial, and Time Reserves to Overloaded Lives, by Richard Swenson. Yes, it deals with money and time. Both of these could be in your 'sweet spot.'

Letting Go of Anger: The Eleven Most Common Anger Styles and What to Do About Them, by Ronald T. Potter-Efron. Good read if you feel you need anger management.

Play: How It Shapes the Brain, Opens the Imagination, and Invigorates the Soul, by Stuart Brown. Brown provides a sweeping look at the latest breakthroughs in our understanding of the importance of play. A cutting-edge blend of neuroscience, biology, psychology, social science, and inspiring human stories of the transformative power of play.

Getting Things Done: The Art of Stress-Free Productivity, by David Allen. Allen's premise is simple: our productivity is directly proportional to our ability to relax.

CONCLUSION

> *"To live a creative life, we must lose our fear of being wrong". - Joseph Chilton Pearce.*

Stress results from an imbalance between our life's interactions and our current ability to rise to the occasion.

Interactions with stress will fluctuate unsteadily. Your stress management will also fluctuate if not prepared. That's called coping. Your coping ability can be creatively raised in strength by fully utilizing the acronyms in this guidebook. You will no longer be subject to unprepared shortcomings and reduced coping ability. Thusly, you can magically and habitually have a reality you can control. You are trying to control three things: motivation, habit, and benefit. Taking in a helpful ally, mate, or spouse in this venture would be of absolutely great benefit.

Motivation: Motivation is defined as a desire to do things. It's a vital ingredient in preparing and reaching goals. Motivation research shows you *can* influence your level of motivation and willpower. Motivation will get you into accord with the acronyms in this guidebook.

Habit: Become a habitual goal setter *daily*. Commit to working on clear beneficial goals everyday, if necessary. You can use the acronym processes leading to imagination, visualization, and creativity as you achieve harmony on life's stage.

Benefit: There is nothing like knowing your accomplishments and achievements. Having helpful friends, partners, or spouses in this venture would be of great benefit as well. Here are a few of your benefits:

- You'll make your life have more zing and energy
- You'll be a more social and entertaining person
- You'll improve memory and recognition
- You'll be more creative and inspiring
- You'll be more perky and alert
- You'll have a boosted immune system
- You'll be much more effective

APPENDIX

Placed in the appendix are short "pin pricks to the imagination" which may aid you in developing how to proceed with your research and planning your action toward enjoying stress.

They were not included in the body of this guide because they tend not to directly feed definition of the acronym strategies.

Hopefully, they will aid you in determining rational ideas from the subliminally irrational ones you may currently carry without a plan.

I: EMOTIONS – BASED IN FACE RECOGNITION

The following research is from the University of Glasgow, published 2014 in *Current Biology*.

Scientific study has traditionally recognized six "classic/basic" emotions: happy, surprised, afraid, disgusted, angry, and sad. Recently, the Glasgow scientists studied people's facial expressions and the emotions they signal by showing people computer-generated facial animations. The observers were to characterize the faces based on those six basic emotions, and found that anger and disgust looked very similar to the observers in the early stages, as did fear and surprise. For example, both anger and disgust share a wrinkled nose, and both surprise and fear share raised eyebrows.

As time went on, the face eventually showed the distinction between the two, but when the emotion first hit, the facial signals are very similar, suggesting, the researchers say, the distinction between anger and disgust and between surprise and fear is socially *not* biologically based.

This leaves us with four "basic" emotions, according to this study: (1) happy; (2) sad; (3) afraid/surprised, and; (4) angry/disgusted. These, the researchers say, are our biologically based facial signals—though distinctions exist between surprise and fear and between anger and disgust. The experiment suggests that these differences developed later, more for social reasons than survival ones.

In conclusion, the research suggests these four emotions are the basic building blocks from which we develop our modern, complex, and emotional stews.

Just think about this for a moment. Is it not interesting that fear and surprise are so biologically linked. By the same token, anger and disgust are biologically linked. If you compared and contrasted these thoughts with stress—you were right if you assumed a correlation.

Yes, unmanaged and out-of-control stress is most certainly an emotional stew! This may be fed when you can't immediately tell if someone in a confrontation is angry or disgusted (at you or themselves). In the same fashion, you can't tell if they are fearful or surprised.

It should be clear; you should therefore buy some time for them and yourself. This is necessary if you want to come to a logical understanding as to exactly what is going on emotionally.

II: LEGITIMATE RIGHTS YOU HAVE

You may want to take note of this list in *The Relaxation & Stress Reduction Workbook,* by Davis, Eshelman & McKay. The following paraphrase analysis explains your legitimate rights:

- You have a right to think of yourself first. For example, you're told not to put yourself before or above others.
- You have a right to make a mistake. For example, *you're told that's shameful.*
- You have a right to be the final judge of your own feelings. For example, you're told that your feelings don't make sense – maybe you are going crazy.

- You have a right to your convictions and processes. For example, you're told shut up and keep your differences to yourself.
- You have a right to change your mind. For example, you're told to be logical and consistent.
- You have a right to protest unfair treatment of any nature. For example, you're told that others have good ideas and it's only polite not to question them.
- You have a right to ask for clarification. For example, you're told not to interrupt and ask questions as this only reveals your own stupidity.
- You have right to negotiate change. For example, you're told things could get worse—don't rock the boat.
- You have a right to feel sad and express pain. For example, you're told to keep it to yourself.
- You have a right to receive formal recognition for your work and achievements. For example, you're told that doing something well is its own reward—don't show off.
- You have a right not to have to justify yourself to others. For example, you're told you should always have a good reason for what you feel and do.
- You have a right to choose not to respond to a situation. For example, you're told to give an answer now and why think about it and put it off.

III: WHERE STRESS HANGS OUT

Telephone: Decide on what times of day you will "bunch" your calls and perform that way. Obviously, you'll need an effective answering system that is friendly sounding—sell yourself. If someone calls during those times, answer.

Unexpected visitors: These unscheduled interruptions may be a central part of your job description and therefore probably manage them fairly well. If not part of your job and/or you are not managing them well, you'll need to make yourself immediately give visitors notice that you are busy and can talk with them later. Maybe you need an appointment system?

Meetings: Are you involved in too many meetings? How many of them are productive and effective? Are they poorly done? Of course, some meetings are very necessary and may be effective. However, for those meetings that are stress hangouts or time wasters, you may have to make interesting proposals for change to your benefit.

Lack of goals and priorities: Maybe you're constantly saying, "Where am I going?" Maybe you're saying, "Where should I start?" Perhaps it's time to make or restore a program or goals making priorities which make good sense.

Garbled communications or bad listening habits: Maybe you have been in a situation where someone is saying, "I'm sure I/you said that!" Good communication has to involve feedback (response). Learn yourself, or teach others, to respond orally with a response which tells the other you heard correctly (or incorrectly) what they said.

Conflict resolution: The following process is useful for effectively managing conflict in your workplace, in relationships, or in other situations where you have an interest in seeking a negotiated solution. These steps won't guarantee an agreement, but they greatly improve the likelihood that the problems can be understood, solutions explored, and consideration of the advantages of a negotiated agreement can occur within a relatively constructive environment. They provide useful strategies to consider that reduce the impacts of stress, fears, and "surprise" factors involved in dealing with conflict.

> 1. "Know thyself," and take care of yourself. 2. Clarify personal needs threatened by the dispute and identify "desired outcomes" from a negotiated process. 3. Take a listening stance into the interaction. "Seek first to understand, then to be understood. Use active listening skills.

> 4. Assert your needs clearly and specifically. Use "I-messages" as tools for clarification and avoid "you-messages", i.e. Instead of saying, "What do you think?" say, "I think . . ." Do not say, "Well, you did this . . ."

5. Approach problem-solving with flexibility. Identify issues clearly and concisely. Generate options (brainstorm), while deferring judgment. Be open. 6. Manage impasse with calm, patience, and respect. Clarify feelings on both sides. Focus on basic needs, interests, and concerns. 7. Build an agreement that works. Review "hallmarks" of an agreement. Implement and evaluate—live and learn.

Procrastination: This often involves indecision. There's only one strategy to avoid procrastination—do the work!

Attempting too much: If you are constantly missing deadlines, you are more than likely doing too much. Possibly you are saying yes to too many things as you have an inability to say no. Possibly you are trying to be too perfectionist instead of being effective.

Personal disorganization: Where did it go—where did I put that? Most certainly you can decide to solve this by using simplicity and the wastebasket.

Untimely or unreliable information: There is no way to avoid folks who spread rumors, false information, hoaxes, and hearsays. All you have to do is double-check information accurately after it's been given to you so it can be used effectively.

IV: LOOKING AT WORRY

You can spend the rest of your life worrying about the future, and no amount of worry will change a thing. Worry is defined as being immobilized in the present time as a result of imagined things that are going or not going to happen. Therefore, if you are developing a life plan, this activity will contribute to a more effective future—that activity is not worry.

Our society and culture fosters and, indeed, encourages worry. Worrying will most likely make you less effective in dealing with the present. Much of what you worry about concerns things over which you have no control.

The collective "worry sheets" of our culture and your own "worry sheet" totaled up will always add up to zero, zip, and nada.

How does my "worry sheet" resemble yours? Try making your own:

- ✓ My children: "I wouldn't be a good parent if I didn't."
- ✓ My health: "If I didn't worry about getting cancer, I might."
- ✓ Dying: "Everybody worries about that!"
- ✓ My job: "I might lose it—I have to worry about it."
- ✓ My companion's (spouse) happiness: "They'll think I don't care."
- ✓ What others may think: "My friends may not like me."
- ✓ Money: "Unless I worry about dollars someday, I'll be broke."
- ✓ Having nothing to worry about: "What is going to happen next?"

In order to slow down and eliminate worry you need to understand at least a couple of things. First of all *why* do you worry? After considering that question, possibly you have come to understand and can accept the fact that you can *choose* not to worry. Secondly, having truly chosen not to worry needlessly, you go into your new days by developing a life plan on paper that will address the positives you wish to pursue.

V: IRRATIONAL IDEAS = STRESS

Working with irrational ideas in your head certainly leads to stress on your mind and body. Do you have something like these in your head?

- ✓ That you must, yes, must, have love or approval from everyone you find significant. Why stress over that?
- ✓ That you must prove yourself to be thoroughly competent, adequate, and achieving. Or a saner, but still foolish version of yourself; that you at least must have competence or talent in some important area.
- ✓ That when people act obnoxiously and unfairly, you should blame and damn them as bad, wicked, or rotten individuals. That won't help!
- ✓ That you have to view things as awful, terrible, horrible, and catastrophic when you're frustrated, treated unfairly, or rejected.

✓ That emotional misery comes from external pressures, and that you have little ability to control or change your feelings. Poor thing!

✓ That if something seems dangerous or fearsome, you must automatically preoccupy yourself and make yourself anxious about it.

✓ That you can more easily avoid facing life difficulties and self-responsibilities rather than doing rewarding forms of self-discipline.

✓ That your past remains all-important, and that because something once strongly influenced your life, it has to keep determining your feelings and behavior today. It's time to be you!

✓ That people and things should turn out better than they do and you must view it as awful and horrible if you do not find good solutions to life's grim realities.

✓ That you can achieve maximum human happiness by inertia and inaction or by passively and committedly pleasing yourself.

CPSIA information can be obtained at www.ICGtesting.com
Printed in the USA
BVOW08*1524030616

450563BV00001B/2/P